COWBO

STEUE FOSTER

COWBOY

By
Ross Santee

Illustrated by the Author

University of Nebraska Press
Lincoln and London

Publishers on the Plains

UNP

First Bison Book printing: 1977

Most recent printing indicated by first digit below:
2   3   4   5   6   7   8   9   10

Library of Congress Cataloging in Publication Data
Santee, Ross, 1889–1965.
  Cowboy.
  Reprint of the ed. published by Grosset &
Dunlap, New York.
  I. Title.
[PZ3.S2287Co8]   [PS3537.A76]   813'.5'2   77–7271
ISBN 0–8032–0931–2
ISBN 0–8032–5867–4 pbk.

Manufactured in the United States of America

For
Shorty Caraway—top hand

CONTENTS

COWBOY

CHAPTER I

Runaway

THE ranch looked like a tiny speck when we first caught sight of it. But as we kept on ridin' closer we could make out the pole corrals. I'll never forget the thrill I got at the sight of them pole corrals an' the tall black-headed puncher standin' in the ranch-house door as we rode up, a-smokin' a cigarette. For this was no farm with a cotton patch an' a bunch of milk-pen cows, but a real cow ranch, just like I'd dreamed about ever since I was a kid.

For I always wanted to be a cow-puncher. As a little kid back on the farm in east Texas I couldn't think of nothin' else. Most kids, I guess, is that-a-way, but they never could knock the idea out of me. That was all farmin' country even then, but once in a while someone would

1

drive a bunch of cattle by our place. I couldn't
have been more than six years old when I follered one bunch off. It didn't make any difference to me that I was the only one afoot. I had
a long stick an' I was busier than a coon dog
drivin' drags. I had an uncle Jim a-livin' down
the road about four miles, who happened to see
me goin' past his place.

"Whatcha doin', kid?" he yells.

"A-punchin' cows," I says.

By promisin' to let me ride old Joe, a pony
that he owned, he finally talked me into goin' on
back home with him.

The next time I left when I was just fourteen.
I got a little further West this trip, but they
brought me back a second time.

A cousin, Fred, who was just my age, an' me
had always planned to go out West when we got
big enough an' go to punchin' cows. Fact is,
when us two was alone we didn't talk of nothin'
else. An' we spent our time a-ridin' all the milk-
pen calves an' a-ropin' at every hog in sight. It
was when dad finally put a stop to ropin' his fat
hogs that me an' Fred decided it was time to
leave. Dad didn't mind so much about the calves
we rode. But he did object to ropin' them fat
hogs of his.

It was on Sundays while the family was at church that me an' Fred got in our biggest licks. Fred mostly spent Sundays at our place, or else I spent the day at his. We always had to go to Sunday School, but we usually made some good excuse for duckin' church.

On this particular day we'd beat it home from Sunday School, an' after ridin' all the calves there was we decided to practice ropin' for a spell. Dad had taken my rope away from me an' hid it some time back. But it wasn't long before we had the clothes-line down an' had a big loop built. Fred was for cuttin' it in two, so's both of us could have a rope. But I knowed that mother, as easy-goin' as she was, would never stand for that.

We practiced on the calves awhile, a-takin' turn about, an' then we drove the work team up an' roped awhile at them. But they was both so gentle they wouldn't even run. *Action* was

what we wanted so we thought about the hogs.
We didn't intend to run 'em much, just a couple
of throws apiece. But Fred accidentally caught
an' old sow by the leg, an' away the whole bunch
went. We s'posed, of course, the loop would
drop right off when Fred turned loose the rope.
But in some way the loop got fouled, an' it never
would come off. We thought of a half a dozen
different schemes. An' finally decided if we run
her long enough the loop was bound to work
loose.

So we circled the hogs until we both was wet
with sweat, an' their tongues was hangin' out.
An' the more we run the critters, the tighter the
blame loop got. At intervals we stopped for
air. An' at last Fred quit. But the thoughts
of dad drivin' in at any time still kept me on
the run. Finally it occurred to Fred that we
might cut the rope, an' with that I beat it for
the house an' got the butcher knife.

As usual with plans that he an' I worked out
I come in for the heavy end. For I was to pick
up the rope an' hold the sow while Fred cut the
critter loose.

The hogs had all got quiet in one corner of the
lot, an' the old sow was layin' down. But the
minute we started towards them they all broke

into a run. We circled them twice before I could
pick up the rope. An' once I managed to get
holt of it I never did turn loose. I've had horses
drag me a lot of times since then. But I've
never been drug through a hog-lot since, a-
wearin' my Sunday clothes. The old sow was
gradually slowin' down, with me draggin' on
the rope. An' just as the folks drove into the
yard Fred managed to cut her loose.

What happened then was what most anybody would expect. The thing wound up by
Fred a-goin' home an' me to the barn with dad.

I didn't get to see Fred again until the next
Sunday. The old sow had died in the mean-
time, an' when the folks kept us both in church
that day we decided it was time to leave. Fred
was to ride over to our place the follerin' Saturday, just as he often did to spend the night. An'
we planned to slip out of the house while the
folks were all asleep.

It was a long old week for me. We'd talked
it over lots of times before, but now that the time
was really set to go I couldn't hardly wait. An'
I was afraid that somethin' might turn up after
all an' Fred wouldn't get to come. But early
Saturday evenin' he come a-ridin' in. An' he
brought two six-shooters of his dad's to take with

us on the trip. Fred said we'd both need guns
out West. I'd always figgered too that a cow-
puncher should have a gun. An' the fact that
the one he give me had a broken spring an'
wouldn't shoot didn't bother me none at all. For
we didn't have any shells for them. We figgered
we'd get them later on.

We cached the guns in the haymow while we
went in to eat. But the minute that supper was
over we beat it for the barn again. An' practiced pointin' them at things around the place
until it got too dark to see. As soon as it was
good an' dark we brought the ladder up from
the orchard an' put it against the window of
my room. My room was on the second floor
an' we had to go through the room where dad
an' mother slept to get up or down the stairs.
I knowed there was no chance of us a-gettin' out
that way for dad slept with both ears cocked.

The folks might have knowed there was somethin' up. For as soon as we got the ladder fixed,
me an' Fred both turned in. As a usual thing
when Fred stayed with me dad made at least
two trips up-stairs before we would quiet down.
But this night they never heard a cheep from
us, for we both was quiet as mice.

It seemed like dad an' mother never would

go to bed. Fred was for slippin' down the ladder while they was both down-stairs. But I knowed the last thing mother done each night was to make the rounds of us kids. An' see how my sisters an' me was gettin' on before she went to bed.

We must have waited two hours. For me an' Fred had quit whisperin'. An' I could hear the old clock tick. An' the barkin' of a neighbor's dog sounded awful lonesome to me. Somehow I didn't feel like talkin' now. Fred was quiet too. I never remember goin' to sleep; but the next thing I heard was dad callin' us, an' it was broad daylight.

Of course, we both felt foolish after all the plans we'd made. But we figgered it out in church that day that we'd leave that afternoon. We'd saddle up after dinner just to take a little ride, an' instead of comin' back that evenin' we'd keep right on our way.

Fred had a good horse an' saddle. I was
ridin' an old pacin' horse called Dan that dad
used to the buggy an' for light work around the
farm. My saddle was one of them old high-
horned things that had hung for years in the
barn. There wasn't no linin' in it, an' the leathers was all curled up. The bridle was one of
them old things with blinders on. But the pair
of California spurs I wore made up for all the
things I lacked. I'd traded with a Mexican
for them.

The sun was mighty warm that day we left.
An' the last thing dad said to me when we rode
off was not to run old Dan. Fred had rolled
both guns inside his coat an' tied it on behind.
I didn't even take a coat for fear dad would
smell a mouse. We didn't do much talkin' the
first half-mile or so. We both was feelin' low.
For my sisters was playin' in the yard, an' the
glimpse I got of mother standin' in the door
as we rode out the gate was most too much for
me.

Down at the second crossroads we met some
kids we knowed, a-battin' flies while they was
waitin' for enough kids to show, so's they could
start a game. As a usual thing me an' Fred
was always the first ones there. For next to

ropin' an' ridin', baseball was our game. Of
course, the kids all thought it queer that we
wouldn't get down an' play an' finally we up
an' told 'em that we was goin' West. We made
'em promise first they wouldn't tell a soul. None
of them would believe us till Fred showed them
both our guns. Them guns we packed put
things in an altogether different light an' Butch
Jones was for goin' along. But Butch was
a whole year younger than us, so we made him
stay at home.

We must have made all of twenty miles that
day. For we rode till after dark. At every
orchard that wasn't too close to the house we
got off an' filled our shirts. We picked out
several likely spots to camp, but we always had
to move on again for some dog would begin to
bark. Finally we turned off in a field, where
there wasn't no house in sight. We was lucky
enough to find water so we turned our horses
loose.

We built a fire in a thicket, where it couldn't
be seen from the road. An' practiced pointin'
our guns at trees an' things till we got tired of
that. An' after eatin' some more of the apples
we decided we'd turn in. Fred had a good
saddle-blanket, so we put his blanket over us,

an' usin' the guns as pillows we slept on my gunny sacks.

We did a heap of talkin' before we went to sleep, mostly to keep our courage up—at least I know I did. An' we both agreed a dozen times there wasn't nothin' in the world that would make us go back home. Finally Fred fell asleep. But I laid a long time blinkin' at the stars, just thinkin' of the folks at home.

We was up an' down a dozen times that night a-pokin' at the fire or tryin' to fix the gunny sacks. For that ground got awful hard. It didn't seem to me as if I'd slept at all. But when I woke up the sun was shinin' in my face, an' it was broad daylight. Fred had the fire a-goin' an' was dryin' himself out. For the dew had been so heavy we both was soakin' wet. Neither of us had much to say. But we eat the rest of the apples. An' ketchin' our horses, we saddled up an' started on our way.

We'd made about fifteen miles, I guess, a-playin' each apple orchard that we passed. But we was both fed up on apples when we come to a little country store at noon. Fred was for buyin' everythin' in sight. But I held him down to sardines an' cheese, as hungry as I was. For we only had six dollars an' there was shells to buy. An' I wasn't sure how much it would take to get my six-shooter fixed.

It was here I pulled a batter, an' come near spillin' all the beans. For I asked the old man in the store if he had .45 shells for sale. I might have knowed they didn't sell ammunition in a country grocery store. An' the minute I spoke about the shells the old man looked me over an' asked where we was from. I started to hem an' haw for I was afraid he might get word to dad. But Fred was quick on the trigger an' give him the name of a town this side of where we lived, an' told him we was goin' down the road a piece to visit folks of ours. That seemed to satisfy the old man in the store. An' as soon as he wrapped us up our stuff we eased outside an' went on down the road.

That night we camped by a little stream with timber along its banks. There was plenty of feed for the horses. An' if we'd only had some decent hooks we might have had fish to eat. Fred rigged up an' outfit by usin' a bent safety-pin. He managed to get two bullheads out where we could look 'em over good, but they fell back in again. We still had plenty of apples, but we was burnt out on them. We sat around the fire awhile, but we was both too low to talk. So

finally we spread our gunny sacks an' slept till
it got light.

We didn't have no breakfast. But we planned
to get some stuff to cook at the first place that
we struck. But it wasn't until two that evenin'
that we come to a little town. Fred was for
goin' to the restaurant an' eatin' one big meal.
But I still had guns an' ammunition on my mind,
an' talked him out of that, by sayin' we could get
things cheaper at the store an' cook the stuff ourselves. An' besides, we had a long old ways to
go, an' we might not get a job the first ranch we
struck.

There was several people in the store when me
an' Fred went in. None of them paid us any
mind except one hombre with a white mustache,
who wore a broad-rimmed hat. I noticed he
looked us over awful close an' listened to what
we said. We finally got our stuff wrapped up,
an' just as we was walkin' out this hombre spoke
to us. He was friendly enough all right. But
I come near passin' out. For when he asked us
where we was from, I noticed he wore a star.

Fred told him the same old yarn he'd told
the old man in the store. But he didn't appear
to be satisfied, an' he asked us the names of our
folks. An' the name of the folks we planned on

visitin'. An' he asked just where they lived.
That sort of had Fred up a stump, for he hemmed
an' hawed around. An' finally this hombre up
an' says, "I think you boys has run off." With
that Fred dove right through the door with me
at his heels. An' Tom Mix in all his movie stunts
never mounted as quick as us kids.

As we rode out of town we both looked back
to see if the sheriff was comin' too. But we
couldn't see nothin' but dust. The first quarter
that we rode Dan made it pretty fast, but he
was gradually slowin' down an' blowin' awful
hard. So I had to pull him up. We jogged
along for a spell an' we'd begun to think we'd
lost this bird. Then all at once we saw him
comin' after us a-ridin' a big bay horse.

Fred was ridin' an awful good pony, an' I
don't think the sheriff ever could have caught
him on that big bay of his. But pore old Dan
was through. For that first quarter had finished
him, but he did the best he could. Fred had been
ridin' alongside of me till the sheriff yelled to
halt. An' then he passed me like a shot an' went
on down the road. Old Dan was runnin' just
as fast as he knowed how. But that wasn't fast
enough. An' I was beatin' a regular tattoo
against his ribs with them California spurs. As

the sheriff kept drawin' closer I flattened out,
for I expected him to shoot. But he finally
rode up alongside of me an' got Dan by the bit.
I wouldn't have been surprised if he had shot
me then. But instead of that he laughed.

As soon as he seen that I was caught Fred
come on back. An' then the sheriff told us that
he had got word from dad to be on the lookout
for two stray kids with guns. It seems when
we didn't come home on Sunday night my dad
had gone huntin' for us. He happened to stop
at Jones's, an' Butch had finally told him that
we had started West. It was then dad had
wired ahead.

It seemed to me as if the whole town was out
when the sheriff brought us back. He put our
horses up at the livery barn an' then he wired to
dad. From here he took us to the jail. An' me
an' Fred was feelin' pretty low, for we expected
he'd lock us up. But after showin' us about the
place an' lookin' awful serious he took us home
with him.

The sheriff didn't do much talkin', but his
wife had plenty to say. An' she asked us didn't
we feel ashamed to worry our mothers that way.
Me an' Fred both said we did. She scolded us
all through supper, but she cooked fried chicken

for us. Man! but that dinner was good. It
was while we was eatin' supper the sheriff got
a wire from dad sayin' him an' Uncle Jim would
come for us an' take us home next day.

We slept that night at the sheriff's house. But
before we went to bed the sheriff had to go up
to town again, so he took us kids along.

Most every one we met was curious. For the
race we made when we left town had stirred the
whole place up. An' whenever anyone asked the
sheriff who we was, he'd look at us an' get serious.
"I'm not real shore," he'd say, "but from the
looks of them guns they was packin' I think
it's Frank an' Jesse James."

CHAPTER II

I Hear My First Coyote

I FELT like a sheep-killin' dog when we got home. An' that one trip of ours cured Fred of all his interest in the West. For Dad an' Uncle Jim come for us next day. Uncle Jim took the horses back with him. But me an' Fred went on the train with dad. The sheriff went with us to the train, an' just before the train pulled out he told us kids we'd better stay at home till we got big enough to make a hand, for punchin' cows was nothin' but hard work. It seems he'd been a cow-puncher himself when he was young. But when he shook hands with dad he says that if it's in the breed to go, there's no use tryin' to keep a kid at home, for he'd left, himself, that way.

Dad never had much to say at any time. An' I s'posed we'd have our usual session in the barn

when we got home. But the only thing he said
about my runnin' off was that I ought to be
ashamed to worry mother the way I had. An'
when mother cried an' said how glad she was to
see me back, it made it tough on me. For what
the sheriff said about it bein' in the breed to go
was right: the thing was always on my mind.
It wasn't as if I wasn't well treated at home.
An' that only made it all the worse on me, for
somehow I had to go.

I had one sister a year older than I was that
I used to tell my troubles to, for no matter what
I told her she'd never tell the folks. I had to
talk to someone, as ever since that trip of ours
Fred was off the West. An' all the kids I talked
to was more interested in baseball. So I finally
up an' told her that I was goin' to leave.

"Don't you run off again," she says, "for just
the other night I heard mother talkin' to dad.
An' dad said next time you wanted to leave he
was goin' to let you go. An' when you tried
the thing awhile an' found out what you was
up against, you'd be glad to come back home."

That put things in an altogether different
light. An' it was only a day or so later dad
spoke to me. We was eatin' supper at the time.
An' without a hint of warnin' he cleared his

throat an' asked me when I planned to go out
West again. I sort of hemmed and hawed
around, for I didn't expect he'd put it up to me
that way. But I says, "Pretty soon."

"Now, don't go runnin' off," he says, "an'
worry your mother the way you did before. For
if you're dead-set on goin' West I'll get you an
outfit an' let you go."

That was all dad ever said, but he more than
made good his word. For he bought me a second-
hand saddle an' a little white pony that one of
the neighbors owned. White Man was what
they called him, an' he wouldn't weigh nine hundred pounds. But I've never owned a horse that
looked as good as he did then.

Now that the thing was really set for me to
go, I couldn't hardly wait. An' I was for bein'
on my way at once. But a neighbor kid of ours
named Charlie Johnson had planned to go out
West an' visit an uncle of his. The uncle lived
on the edge of the cow country. An' the folks
figgered it would be better if I rode that far with
him. For Charlie was two years older an' harmless as a mouse.

Dad gave me forty dollars to go with the two
I had, an' he said that ought to run me until I
got a job.

"Now, don't go a-layin' out," he says, "an' coyote along the way, but stop at some farm-house an' spend the night, an' pay for what you get. We'll be glad to see you when you get ready to come home." With that he ups an' shakes hands with me, just as if I was a man. My sisters all just stood around, an' I sort of grinned at them. But mother called me in the house to say good-by to her. It was just as well she did, I guess. For I was no cowboy leavin' home to her, but a little red-nosed kid.

"Be a good boy," was all she said. But she held me mighty close. I saw her again as we rode out the gate, still standin' in the doorway a-smilin' through her tears. My sisters waved to us as long as we was in sight, an' we waved back to them. For as long as the farmhouse was in view I kept a-lookin' back.

We both was pretty quiet the first few miles or so. But the fact that I was really headed West at last soon had me perkin' up. Charlie got off his horse an' filled his shirt at the first orchard that we struck. But I was burnt out on apples, so I opened up the lunch. Mother had fixed a lunch for us that was all White Man could pack. We was takin' the same old road that me an' Fred had took, an' I told Charlie

of things that me an' Fred had said an' done on our other western trip.

"Fred don't know what he's missin'," Charlie says.

"You bet he don't," says I. "But after all it's probably just as well he stayed at home. For anyone who would get burnt out on just one trip would never make a cowboy anyway."

But just the same I wished that Fred was along. An' when we come to the place where me an' Fred had camped the first night out, I took Charlie into the field an' showed him the thicket where us two kids had slept.

Charlie didn't get het up the way Fred an'
I always did. But by the time he rode with me
a week he was for passin' up his uncle's place
an' goin' on with me. For anyone to have heard
me talk would have thought I owned the West.
Mebbe it was just as well I didn't know some
of the things that I was up against. For I pictured things in a mighty rosy light, an' it never
occurred to me but what most anyone who owned
a cow ranch would give a kid a job.

Some days we made most all of forty miles,
an' then again we loafed along an' let our horses
graze. Most of the farmers where we stopped
an' spent the night wouldn't take a cent from
us. In one way we was like cowboys. For we
was free an' easy with the money that we had.
We stopped at every store we passed an' bought
candy an' such truck. Except the one that me
an' Fred was in when the sheriff jumped us out.
Somehow, I didn't have the nerve to stop in there
again, an' I was for ridin' right through the town.
But we hadn't gone a block before someone
yelled at us:

"Hello, Jesse James!"

Shore enough it was the sheriff, but we didn't
run this time.

"Runnin' off again?" he says with a twinkle

in his eyes. He knowed very well we wasn't,
or we'd have rode around his town. "Got a new
pardner, so I see." An' then he says, "Where's
Frank?" I didn't know who he meant at first,
till he laughed an' asked for Fred.

He took us both up home with him an' had
us spend the night. Fried chicken must have
been a steady thing at the sheriff's house. For
his wife cooked it again. An' when we left next
mornin' she packed a lunch for us. She didn't
think much of our trip an' she wasn't slow to
speak her mind. For she says that Fred was
a right smart boy to stay at home an' not go to
trackin' off on a wild-goose chase.

"My land," she says, "what can your paw
an' maw be thinkin' of to let you go this way?"
Naturally, this didn't set so well with me an' I
told her I was goin' on fifteen. "My land!" she
says again, a-raisin' both hands. "You're nothin' but a child."

The sheriff didn't do much talkin', an' I guess
he figgered pretty much like dad. He seemed to
think that we'd be comin' back that way 'fore
long, for when he bid us kids good-by he says
that any time we come through town to stop
an' stay with him.

The days was warm an' sunny. An' the miles

kept rollin' by. There was plenty of feed for
the horses. An' they both was lookin' fine. At
times we grazed them for hours, when we come
to a likely place. An' any time we found water
that was deep enough we got off an' took a
swim. An' I always washed my saddle-blankets.
For dad had always told me that a man who
used clean blankets seldom hurt a horse's back.
An' he always maintained further that anyone
who rode a sore-backed horse wasn't fit to hold
a job.

We rode two weeks, I guess, before it finally
occurred to us that we should wash our clothes.
But once the idea come to us, we acted on it at
once. The first water we struck happened to
be a little dirt tank in a field alongside the road.
Some cows was standin' in the water at one end,
but that didn't bother us. Nor the fact that
the water wasn't over three feet deep, an' that
it was the color of mud.

We didn't have any soap, but if we'd had a
ton of soap it wouldn't have done us any good.
We peeled our shirts an' overalls, an' started in
to work. But the more we scrubbed an' sloshed
our clothes around the dirtier they got. An'
after rilin' all the water in the tank we finally
gave it up. We spread our clothes on the ground

to dry. But even to us kids the washin' wasn't what we called a big success. Fact is the washin' was such a disappointment we never washed our clothes again until we got to Charlie's uncle's.

The further West we got, the better the country looked to me. The days was warm an' sunny, an' the nights was clear an' cold. The farms was few an' far between, an' there wasn't many trees, an' the country stretched away for miles as level as a floor.

I wished for Fred a lot of times, for Charlie was high an' low by turns. One day he was for goin' on with me, an' next day he was for goin' on home again. I'll admit at times my plans was rather wild. I was for goin' on to Arizona now, an' never goin' home again till I owned a cow outfit that was all my own. Then I'd go back in style. I could even see the kids a-turnin' out as I rode down the street, an' me a-wavin' to the ones I knowed.

Of course, I'd still ride White Man. But I'd have a new saddle all covered with pretties, an' silver-mounted spurs; an' I'd let Fred ride him up an' down the road. An' then again I wouldn't be real shore about ridin' White Man back. Of course, I'd never sell him. I'd just keep him at the ranch.

I figgered it would be nice to ride a horse that no one else could ride. An' I could see the kids a-gapin' as he bucked down the street, with me a-settin' on his back as easy as you please. It was times like that I wished for Fred, for Charlie had a way of snubbin' me up short. Right in the middle of some plan that mebbe he was included in he'd up an' ask me some fool question an' bring me back to earth.

The night before we got to his uncle's place we both laid out, for we missed the farm where we had planned to spend the night. We rode for an hour after it got dark, but there was no moon, an' it was so dark we couldn't tell just where we was, so we finally decided to camp. I happened to have some stuff to eat tied on behind. An' we was settin' pretty, so I thought. But the party was spoiled for Charlie 'cause we didn't have nothin' to drink. We had watered our horses just before dark an' watered out ourselves. But to hear him talk he was choked for a drink, an' after I'd listened to him for a while I began to get thirsty myself.

We hobbled the horses out, for we was in the middle of a great big flat an' there wasn't no fence in sight. An' after eatin' what sardines an' cheese I had, we decided we'd turn in. We both had plenty of saddle-blankets, an' except for the fact the cheese had made me thirsty, too, an' Charlie had nothin' but drinkin' water on his mind, we got a pretty good night's sleep. Towards mornin', though, we both froze out for it got pretty cold. There wasn't nothin' we could find to burn, so we got up an' walked around. We forgot we was thirsty, tryin' to keep warm.

About noon next day we finally come to where Charlie's uncle lived. His aunt cooked all the beef an' frijole beans that we could eat an', man! but it was good.

His place was just on the line between Texas an' New Mexico. He run some cattle on the

open range. But the fact that he did some farmin' too an' wore hob-nailed shoes instead of boots
sort of spoilt the place for me. I was for goin'
on next day. But he insisted that I stay an'
rest my pony up, for the first cow-ranch, he said,
was fifty miles west of there. That only made
me squirm the more. I was rarin' to be on my
way. I'd seen enough farmin' country in the
past six weeks to do me for the rest of my life.

I stayed with them three days, an' Charlie's
aunt washed up an' mended all our clothes.
Charlie just sort of hung around the house, but
I rode with his uncle John. One day when I
was ridin' out with him he showed me some
cattle with the outfit's brand that was fifty miles
west of him. An' it gave me an awful thrill when
he told me there wasn't a fence or house to be
seen in all that fifty miles. He told me all he
knowed about the ranch, for he'd been there
lots of times. Fact is, we talked so much about
the place that Charlie decided to go on with me.
At first his aunt objected some, but Charlie's
uncle figgered it would do him good.

"Where anyone is curious about a thing," he
says, "they might as well find out."

Charlie's uncle had worked as a cowboy some,
an' at night he told us yarns while we was settin'

around the fire. I never missed a word he said, an' even then I wondered how a man who had lived like that would be satisfied to farm. An' every night before the family went to bed I'd slip outside. For there was somethin' about this country that made me want to be alone.

The night before we left there was a new moon in the sky. The stars was crackin' overhead like fireflies in a great big bowl, an' as I set a-starin' off acrost the flat I heard my first coyote howl. I know there's lots of punchers cuss their noise, an' say they sneak around. But it's always been music in my ears. An' that night as I set there starin' off acrost the flat I wished that I could answer them.

Charlie's uncle staked us to an old canteen. He said we'd find water on the way, but we might as well pack the thing, for we was apt to get pretty dry. His aunt fixed us up a lunch, an' we pulled out next mornin' long before it started breakin' light. Fact is, we rode two hours before it got light enough for us to see, an' we was both so hungry by that time we stopped an' eat our lunch. It started in drizzlin' rain just after it broke light, an' Charlie was for goin' back. But I talked him out of it by sayin' we must be nearly half-way there.

Charlie's uncle John said we'd strike a wagon road about half-way an' once we struck this road we couldn't miss the place, for it led right to the ranch. Charlie started lookin' for the road before we had gone ten miles. An' he dealt me misery before we come to it by sayin' we was lost.

"You don't know what would happen," Charlie says, "if we don't find the road. We might get lost an' starve to death before we find the place. What do you s'pose would happen if one of our horses broke a leg? We're in a wild country now with wolves an' things around."

I figgered we'd find the place all right. But wolves was somethin' I'd never thought about. I knew that coyotes was harmless. But from the way Charlie put it a wolf was somethin' else again. An' the fact that we was soakin' wet didn't help my feelin's none.

We finally struck the wagon road. An' I figgered everything was all right now. But Charlie insisted that we was goin' back the way we'd started from. This was the first I knowed it, but he was turned around. We hadn't seen the sun all day, but directions was somethin' that never bothered me an' I figgered that I was right. Charlie was two years older than me an' taller by a head, but anyone to have heard him talk would have thought he was four years old.

"We're lost," he says, "an' you're a-goin' the wrong way down the road. If we both starve to death out here it's goin' to be your fault." Yes, he was a cheerful cuss, all right. At times I sort of wondered, but I still kept thinkin' I was right. But to hear him givin' up the head as we rode down the road you'd have thought I was leadin' him to his death.

Finally we spied the ranch. At first it was nothin' but a speck. An' it wasn't until we got close enough to make out the buildings an' the pole corrals that he admitted that I was right. Even then he laid on me just like a heavy stone. At last here was the real cow-ranch just like I'd dreamed about, but even the sight of a real cow-ranch didn't raise his feelin's none.

"What'll we do," says Charlie, "if there ain't nobody home?"

CHAPTER III

The Punchers Tell a Few

IT was late that evenin' when we rode into the
ranch. Us kids was soakin' wet an' nearly
starved, but we set there on our horses a-starin'
at the place until the tall puncher spoke.

"You boys turn loose," he says, "an' come on
in an' eat. You can put your ponies in that
little trap, an' you'd better put your saddles in
the shed, for it's pretty wet out here."

He showed us where to put our stuff, an' as
we follered him inside I never missed a thing
he wore. From his high-heeled boots an' overalls to that high-crowned Stetson hat. The overalls I'd always seen an' wore had bibs an' shoul-
der-straps. But these of his come only to his
waist. He wore them turned up at the bottom,
an' they had narrow stove-pipe legs. It didn't
surprise me none to see the big hat an' high-
heeled boots, for I'd always figgered that was
what a cowboy wore. But I made up my mind

first chance I got I'd ditch the overalls I had
an' get a pair like his.

The outfit had finished supper, an' the room
was full of smoke. At the end of the long table
where they eat four cowboys an' the cook was
playin' cards. An' over in one corner of the
room some more was shootin' dice. There must
have been fifteen punchers in the place. Some
was settin' on their heels around the room just
smokin' cigarettes. One puncher who didn't look
to be much older than me was workin' on a saddle. Another one alongside of him was braidin' a rawhide rope. I figgered he must own the
place, for his hair was white as snow. Some of
them nodded to us when we come in, but most
of them didn't speak.

It was the tall black-headed puncher that
cooked somethin' for us to eat. I follered him
into the kitchen. For everything seemed strange
to me, an' there was somethin' friendly about
this tall black-headed guy although he didn't talk.
There was plenty of frijole beans already cooked.
But he made more coffee an' fried steak an'
cooked more bread for us. It was the first time
I'd ever seen anyone 'cept a woman cook. But
he made biscuits an' had them in the stove as
quick as mother could.

As soon as he got this stuff all on he squatted
on his heels an' rolled another cigarette. At intervals he looked inside to see how the bread
was comin' on, or mebbe he'd chunk the fire with
dried cow-chips from a gunny sack. But he
never said a word. There was a thousand questions on my mind that shore was eatin' me. An'
I finally up an' asked him if the old white-headed
man was the owner of the ranch. He shook his
head an' took a big pull at his cigarette. "Dad's
just a hand," he says.

Charlie's uncle John had told me the foreman's
name was Steve, so I asked him which one of
them was him. He took another long pull on his
cigarette. "I am," was all he says. He was
friendly enough all right in spite of the fact that
he was mighty sparin' with his talk. I wanted
to go to work an' I figgered that now was as
good as any to hit him for a job.

"If you'd have come a few days earlier," he
says, "I might have put you on."

"I want to work," I says, "an' I'm willin' to
do most anything."

"You're welcome to stay an' rest your pony
up," he says, "but the outfit's full-handed now."

When I asked him about the outfits further
west he said he didn't know. But he thought

that work was pretty scarce at them, unless a man was a real cow-hand. I didn't know it at the time, but he was tryin' to spare my feelin's with his talk. For he could have told me easy enough that there wasn't nothin' around a cow outfit that I was fit to do. At other outfits where I stopped they always told me the same old thing—if I'd have dropped in just a few days earlier they might have put me on. But instead of me a-realizin' that I knew nothin' of punchin' cows, I thought the reason I was jinxed was that every time I rode up to a ranch I was always a few days late.

I helped Steve with the dishes after Charlie an' me had eat. An' then we all went into the room where the other punchers was. Steve parked himself on his heels again. An' we set down alongside of him. For there was somethin' friendly about him—if he didn't have nothin' to say. An' the talk of the other punchers was all so strange to me. I couldn't foller them. It seems a puncher named Bill Wilson had broke the dice game up. He was a runty feller with curly hair an' one missin' tooth in front. An' instead of the overalls that most of the punchers wore he had on a pair of khaki pants that was tucked inside his boots. An' he wore the big-

gest hat an' pair of spurs I'd ever seen before.
Dad had quit braidin' on his rope an' was settin' in the poker game. For they had broke
the cook, it seems. He was the only man inside
the room except us kids that wasn't wearin'
boots an' spurs. An' the flour sack he used for
an apron was still tied around his waist.

The room was a long, low-roofed affair with
pictures tacked up around the walls. Most of
them was from the Police Gazette, an' there was
lots of naked women. But one picture was a
page from "Life." It showed a bunch of city
fellers shootin' at a cowboy's feet, an' underneath
it says, "A Tenderfoot in New York." Next to
it was a drawin' by Charlie Russell of a pitchin'
horse, a calendar from a saddle house, an' then
more naked women. Some six-shooters with
cartridge-belts, an' some yeller slickers hung
from nails around the wall. Along with odds
an' ends of rope, some wore-out pants, a pair
of leather chaps, a coat or two, an' some sacks
of dirty clothes. In one corner of the room was
piled some bed-rolls, all tied an' corded up. An'
in another corner three 30-30's stood.

A red-haired puncher told some yarn about the
last time he'd been to town. I couldn't foller all
of it. But it seems he met some pretty girl.

An' the punchers all started laughin' when he
told them how he left town. An' then Bill Wilson told us about a trip he'd made to Chicago
once, when he went up there with a load of stock.

"After I turned the cattle over," he says, "I
had a couple of hours yet before my train pulled
out. So I thought I'd see the town. I mounted
the first street-car that come by, for I'd never
rode one of them before. It was about five in
the evenin' when I mounted her, an' everythin'
went fine at first. For I was seein' lots of things
that was new to me. But people kept gettin'
on the car till we was packed just like sardines.
I didn't mind at first for I was sittin' by a window, a-takin' in the sights. I never saw so many
people in my whole life. For they swarmed out
of every canyon that we passed just like a bunch
of ants. I thought at first there was a fire some
place. But when I asked the feller sittin' next
to me he laughs an' says they was comin' home
from work. So I didn't talk to him no more.

"We rode for an hour, mebbe. An' I begun
to figger if I was goin' to ketch my train I'd
better be gettin' off. But there wasn't no chance
of that. For the car was still jam full. I didn't
know what to do, so I set there for mebbe thirty
minutes more. When finally this feller settin'

next to me, he up an' fights his way right through the crowd an' yells he's gettin' off. I took my cue from him an' stayed right at that hombre's heels. For he went right through them people like an old steer through the brush. I lost two buttons off my coat but I made it off the car.

"I didn't have no idea where the depot was so I finally asked a cop. An' he told me it was only two blocks off an' pointed the thing right out to me. I figgered I was jake. For I'd seen lots of the city an' had a good street-car ride. But when I got into the depot they told me it wasn't the place. I never had no idea there was more than one depot in the town. An' I only had twenty minutes to ketch my train. I didn't know what to do. For I knowed I'd never find the other depot now. But the feller in the ticket

place tells me to take a cab. The feller that
drove the cab was nothin' but a kid, but he shore
did know the town. I've been there once since
then. But that one trip cured me of tryin' to
run around. For next time as soon as I turned
the cattle over I rolled my tail for home."

The red-haired puncher finally looked at me
an' Charlie as if he'd just discovered us an' asked
where we was from.

"East Texas," says Charlie.

"That so?" the redhead says. "Did they dip
you boys when you crossed the line from Texas
into New Mexico?"

"No," Charlie says; an' then I spoke up an'
asked him what they should dip us for.

"Ticks," the redhead says. "You boys may
not know it, but you have broke the law. For
it says that all people comin' from Texas to
New Mexico must be dipped 'long with their
stock."

"Uncle John never told us anything like that
an' I guess he'd know," says Charlie.

"Your uncle John knows well enough," Red
says, "an' if they find out he sent you boys acrost
the line without dippin' you, they can send your
uncle up. Of course, I wouldn't say a word
myself. For I wouldn't make trouble for no

man. But if the law was to find out that we took you in, they could make it hard on us. Of course, I'm just a-workin' here myself an' I guess that's up to Steve."

Charlie an' I both looked at Steve. I had some doubts of Red. But anythin' Steve said went down with me for he was the foreman of the ranch. Steve pulled a long time at his cigarette an' finally he says, "That's right; I'd hate to make trouble for his uncle John. An' I'd hate to see these boys go off to jail. But if we dip them here at the ranch we can get around the law."

"We ain't got ticks," I says.

"How do you know?" says Red. "For all you care, the whole outfit might get lousy as a pet coon with them, just because of you two kids."

Finally I says, "All right." For I figgered if it had to be done we might as well get it over with. But Steve says as long as we've put it off this long we could wait till tomorrow mornin'.

From ticks they switched the conversation to skunks. "I ain't afraid of them," I says, "for I've trapped lots of skunks at home."

"Kid," says Bill Wilson, speakin' up, "you ain't never seen no skunks like the kind they got

out here. Of course, these skunks out here smells
pretty much the same as the ones you're speakin'
of, but these out here goes mad."

I remembered of hearin' of hydrophobia
skunks some place an' I sort of looked at Steve.

He took a long pull on his cigarette. "I
reckon it's so," he says. "But there ain't as
many of them around the ranch right now as
there is at other times. It must be goin' on six
months now since that last man here was bit."

"Funny thing," says Bill Wilson. "I never
could figger how that skunk ever got inside the
house, unless he come in at the window, an' this
feller that he bit had only been here just a day.
He was sleepin' in the other room right next to
here, where you kids will sleep tonight. Me
an' Red was sleepin' in this room, an' first thing
we knowed that anythin' was wrong we heard
him yellin'; an' here he come a-tearin' right
through this room an' right on out the door,
a-slobberin' at the mouth. We was shore scairt
all right."

"I'll say we was," says Red.

"What did you do?" we says.

"Well, there wasn't much that we could do
till it got daylight. But me an' Red set up
the rest of the night with our guns right in our

hands, for we was afraid he might come back
at any time an' bite either me or Red, or mebbe
bite the both of us. But as soon as it got light
we saddled up an' cut for sign. We finally
jumped him out, but we couldn't any more ketch
him on a horse than we could fly. But finally,
after we run him nearly half a day, we managed
to get close enough that Red could get a shot
at him."

We looked at Red. "What did you shoot
him for?" we says.

Red shook his head. "I never hated to kill
a man as much as I did him. But we couldn't
have him runnin' loose that way, for he might
bite someone."

I don't know how Charlie felt. But things
was comin' too fast for me. At first I figgered
it was a lie an' then again I didn't know.

After Bill Wilson an' Red had finished their
yarn they went outside the house. But in a
little while they come on back an' went to playin'
cards. There was no one else playin' now 'cept
them two. An' no one paid any hed to them
till they started talkin' loud. But as soon as
Bill started cussin' him Red made a grab for
his gun. An' with that Bill dropped his cards
an' made a run towards us kids.

That was enough for Charlie an' me, for as soon as we saw Red's gun we made a break for the door. As we hit the door we heard a shot, but we never did look back. An' just as we heard them shoot again, we hit the rope they had stretched outside an' we both went flat to the ground. It was only a second till we was up again an' on our way. But in that one second Charlie had run clear off from me. They was still shootin' from the door, so finally I laid down an' flattened out as flat as I could get. An' as I laid there wonderin' how many had been killed I heard some puncher laugh. At first I didn't get it an' I wondered what he meant. For shootin' a man in a card game was no laughin' thing to me.

An' then I heard another puncher say, "Didn't that skinny one run!" Then another puncher spoke. "That little one never throwed off none that I could see." An' then the whole bunch laughed.

When I finally got it through my head that the thing was all a joke I come on back an' tried to laugh it off. But there's no denyin' I was scairt, an' they had to hunt Charlie up.

The whole bunch set around an' laughed when we got inside the house. Finally Steve said it must be gettin' late an' he reckoned he'd turn in. He took us kids in the other room an' showed us where we'd sleep. When he struck a match I could see beddin' rolls layin' all about the room. Steve finally uncorded a roll for us. An' while Charlie struck matches so we could see he helped me spread it out. As soon as Steve got us kids fixed up he set down on a bed alongside of ours on the floor an' started pullin' off his boots.

It wasn't long before I heard Steve snore. But me an' Charlie was too spooky to go to sleep. For each time we started dozin' off, some puncher come in to bed. Each puncher struck a match to find his bed, an' most of them smoked a cigarette before they began to snore. The rain was still patterin' on the roof an' it was pretty stuffy in the room. But the longer I laid the wider awake I got. An' I finally asked Charlie, when they dipped us for ticks next day if he thought they'd dip us with all our clothes on.

"I don't know," he says, "for I ain't never seen nobody dipped for ticks before."

"Do you believe the yarn about the skunks?" I says.

"We're in a wild country now," he says, "an' we can expect most anythin'."

"I don't believe it anyway," I says. An'
Charlie didn't say no more. But as soon as I
figgered they was all asleep I got up an' shut
the door an' put the window down.

CHAPTER IV

In the Cow Country

IT was breakin' light when Charlie an' me woke up. All of the punchers had dressed an' gone 'cept Bill Wilson. Bill was sittin' up in bed a-pullin' on his pants an' smokin' a cigarette. "Mornin', kids," he says. An' when Bill asked who put that window down, Charlie said it wasn't him so I admitted that I had.

"You done just right," says Bill. "I don't see how we all forgot to put it down. An' if it hadn't been for you we might all of us have been bit last night."

I didn't know whether he was spoofin' me or not, for he never cracked a smile. But when

Charlie an' me went in where the rest of the
outfit was they all started kiddin' me.

Breakfast wasn't ready yet, but the whole outfit as near as I could see was playin' the coffee-
pot. Finally the cook says "Chuck." An' every
man set down to eat 'cept Steve. I finally asked
Bill Wilson if he was sick. But he says that
Steve never eat no breakfast 'cept coffee and
cigarettes.

We had steak an' frijole beans again, an'
stewed fruit, an' hot biscuits that wasn't as good
as Steve had cooked for us two kids the night
before. There was no butter, but instead of it
the punchers used some kind of syrup they called
lick. I asked Bill Wilson why they used canned
milk. An' when he told me there wasn't a milk
cow on the place, I figgered that he was kiddin'
me again. But later the cook told me that it
was so. He said the outfit was on the move
so much it wouldn't bother to get one up. An'
he says in all the cattle the outfit run, there
wasn't a milk cow in the bunch.

Just as we finished eatin' Dad an' Red come
in. For them two had been on wrangle, an'
they'd just brought the horses in.

Charlie wiped the dishes for the cook. But
I follered the outfit to the corral an' watched

them ketch their horses. There must have been all of two hundred in the bunch an' they dodged an' milled around. But once they felt the rope around their neck they walked right out as gentle as could be. Except the one Bill Wilson rode. It took three punchers to drag him out. He was a big iron-gray. He struck at Steve with both front feet, when he went down the line an' caught him by both ears. An' Steve chewed on one of them while Bill put on the hackamore an' laced his saddle on. As Bill eased up in the saddle the big gray sort of sagged till his belly almost touched the ground. An' Steve kept chewin' on one ear an' sort of wooled his head around till Bill says to turn him loose.

Dad had drove the other horses out of the corral an' shut the gate. But instead of goin' on with them he waited to see the fun. For the moment Steve turned the big gray loose, he hung his head an' went into the air with Bill. I'd seen lots of colts that I thought bucked, an' I'd rode colts at home I thought was pitchin' hard. But when I saw this big gray horse turn on with Bill I knowed that all the colts I'd ever seen an' tried to ride had just crow-hopped around. The big gray was bawlin' now an' he was shore a-jumpin' crooked. But Bill kicked

him every jump he made, an' when Bill fanned
him with his hat I'd have give' anything in the
world if I could ride like that.

Finally the big gray throwed up his head an'
started trottin' around the big corral. An' after
he trotted round a time or two, a puncher opened
the gate. The gray an' Bill was both a-breathin'
hard as they rode out the gate. An' when Bill
grinned an' waved his hand at me as he rode
out, I realized there was lots of things about a
horse I didn't know. But I made up my mind
I'd learn.

Before the outfit left I asked Steve how far
it was to the next cow-ranch. Steve told me I'd
better stay a few days more an' rest my pony
up. But when I told him I wanted to work,
an' it was up to me to find a job, he says the
next place is about thirty miles northwest of
there. An' for me to take the first trail to the
right an' foller it until I come to a dry lake-
bed that was about half-way. I couldn't miss
it then. I had a few dollars left, but when I
offered to pay him for me an' Charlie stayin'
overnight he only laughed at me.

"Button!" he says. "They don't do things like
that around a ranch. Any man who is huntin'
work is always welcome to stop. I'm sorry that

I can't put you on. But there's only a few things like wranglin' horses an' such as that a kid can do, an' Dad's a-doin' that."

"Another thing," he says, an' then Steve sort of smiled. "Don't believe everything that a cowboy says or they'll try an' deal you misery." An' with that he says, "So long."

I stood an' watched them ridin' off, with Steve up in the lead. An' as they finally topped a little rise an' disappeared I'd have give' most anything I knowed if I had been along.

There was plenty of cold steak an' biscuits left. But the cook never offered to pack no lunch. An' what's more he never said a word when Charlie an' me rode off. I figgered he must be swelled about somethin' that we'd said or done. But later on, after I'd been out awhile, I found he was only runnin' true to form.

It was sunup when we left the ranch, an' the day was clear an' bright. Naturally, I was disappointed that we hadn't got a job. For I liked Steve as well as anyone I'd ever seen. I'd have liked to work for him. Fact is I liked them all, except the cook. But I wasn't low for very long. For the sun felt good on my back. An' it was good to be on White Man's back again. An' wasn't we headin' for another ranch?

But Charlie was feelin' low. He never had nothin' to say until we come to where the trail forked off. An' then he pulled up his horse an' said he was goin' back to his uncle's place an' he wanted me to go too. I tried to talk him out of it, but Charlie's mind was set.

"You're in a wild country now," he says, "an' you've never seen folks as tough as these before. An' besides they may not give you a job when you get to this other ranch."

I had to admit that he was right about me gettin' a job. But if I didn't get one at the next place there was plenty of other ranches. An' I didn't agree about the punchers bein' tough. They might be different from any folks I'd ever been around before, but they just suited me.

"I'm two years older than you," he says, "an' you don't have no idea what you're up against. You're in a wild country now, an' some cowboy might even kill you just to get your horse an' saddle."

I figgered that White Man was as good a horse as ever lived an' I wouldn't blame no cowboy for wantin' him. But I didn't believe no cowboy was quite as tough as that. An' after seein' the rigs that Steve an' the other punchers rode I had my doubts of anyone a-wantin' my saddle.

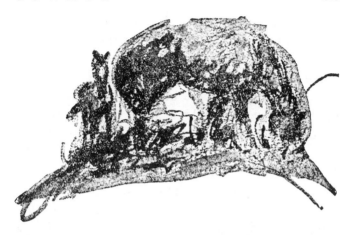

Fact is, I knowed that most of them wouldn't have took it as a gift. Finally I says to Charlie that if he wasn't comin' on with me I was goin' on myself.

"Your folks won't never see you again," he says, an' with that he begun to bawl. That was too much for me, for I was feelin' pretty low myself at the idea of goin' on alone. An' I turned White Man up the trail, for I figgered that Charlie would change his mind an' come along with me. But when I looked back at him again he was ridin' down the road.

I kept a-lookin' back an' finally he stopped his horse, so I pulled White Man up a-thinkin' he might turn around an' come on back. An'

I s'pose he figgered that I might change my mind, for he finally went down the road again.

Just before he disappeared he stopped his horse again, an' I pulled White Man up an' waved to him to come on back. He set there on his horse for quite a spell, then finally he went on. I watched him until he was out of sight. An' I never saw him again. But Charlie made it home all right. For several years later, in a letter I got from home, among other news they wrote that Fred an' Charlie Johnson were both married now an' both was doin' well. I didn't know the girl Fred married, for her folks had come there after I left home. But Charlie had married a girl who lived just north of us, the only girl I had ever liked.

I finally come to the dry lake-bed. An' that evenin' I come to the ranch. It looked much the same as the one I'd left, with its long, low ranch-house an' windmill an' the same kind of pole corrals. But there was only one puncher there. He looked a little bit like Steve, for he was tall an' slim, but he limped some when he walked. He said his name was Jake, he was breakin' horses at the ranch an' stayin' by himself. He said the rest of the oufit was out on the range some place, an' the wagon wasn't due at the ranch for another couple of weeks. I stayed with Jake three days, for he was mighty glad to have someone around. An' he urged me to stay until the outfit come.

"It's been six weeks," he says, "since I've had someone to auger with." But when I asked Jake about a job he said he didn't know.

"I'm just workin' here myself, the foreman's with the wagon. But when they get back here the work is through, an' they'll be layin' some punchers off." I knew that let me out. But Jake was so glad to have someone around he didn't tease me none. I was sort of tired that night, but Jake kept on a-talkin' after my head begun to bob.

In the mornin' he cooked biscuits an' steak. An' we had frijole beans again. An' while Jake wrangled horses I washed an' wiped the dishes an' tried muckin' out the place. But I finally gave that up. For the ranch looked like a boar's nest as near as I could see. Jake evidently hadn't used a broom in the six weeks he'd been alone. An' as soon as he come in with the horses I decided if it suited Jake the way it was, it would be all right with me.

Jake drove about twenty horses into the corral—all broncs, he said they was. They had all

been rode a few saddles, but most of them still
bucked, except one little bay that was the gen-
tlest thing I'd ever seen. Jake thought a lot of
him. He had only been rode two saddles, an'
he had never humped his back. Jake topped him
off, an' after he had trotted him around the corral awhile he let me get on his back.

"You're on a real horse now," he says. "He's
goin' to make a top if some fool puncher don't
spoil him after I turn him in."

Jake let me ride the little bay awhile an' then
he pulled his saddle off an' turned the horse out.

"Mebbe you'd like to try this one, kid," says
Jake, a-shakin' out a little loop. He finally
dabbed it on a little roan, an' the fur begun to
fly. For the roan horse bolted an' dragged Jake
all around the corral. I tried to help Jake out
by draggin' on the rope. "You'd better get on
the fence," says Jake, "for this one is pretty
rank."

Jake finally got a dally around the snubbin'
post in the center of the corral, an' the roan
horse soon choked down. Jake let me hold the
dallies while he slipped the hackamore on, an'
then Jake let the roan get to his feet, but he still
fought so Jake slipped a loop around both front
feet an' flattened him again.

"I'll give him some time to think it over now,"

says Jake, a-rollin' a cigarette. But when Jake
let him up he begun to fight again. So Jake
promptly jerked his front feet out from under
him an' flattened him again. But when the roan
got to his feet again he made another fight, so
Jake tied up one hind foot an' the roan was
helpless now.

Jake spent at least twenty minutes now, just
foolin' with the little roan. He rubbed his nose
an' slapped his back an' sides, an' he must have
put the blanket on his back an' took it off a
hundred times. He even slapped him with it
until finally the roan quit shakin', an' then Jake
put the saddle on. But the minute he pulled up
his latigo, the roan horse humped his back till
the saddle cocked way up behind. Jake laughed
at that, an' he said the way the saddle set a dog
could crawl under the skirts.

Jake rolled another cigarette an' let the roan
horse stand. "Want to try him, kid?" he says.
I wanted to learn an' I figgered that now was as
good as any time to start. But when I said I
did, Jake told me I'd better not.

"He's too much horse for a kid," he says, "an'
you'd better wait awhile. Some peelers would
get a great kick out of watchin' you git bucked
off, but I don't want to get you hurt."

Jake pulled awhile on his cigarette an' wooled

the roan around. First thing I knowed the ropes
was off, an' Jake had gathered himself an ear an'
was settin' in the saddle. The roan didn't even
know that he was loose when Jake slipped acrost
his back. But he wasn't long in findin' it out,
an' when he did he let him know it.

It looked like a mighty simple thing to me
a-standin' there on the ground. Jake might have
been sittin' in a rockin'-chair for all it bothered
him. I never missed a move he made, from the
time he gathered an ear an' slipped into the
saddle until he got holt of the ear again an'
stepped down to the ground. Jake rolled another cigarette an' let the roan horse rest awhile.
An' after he spent ten minutes, just gettin' on
his back an' gettin' off, he had me open the gate.

Jake wasn't gone but a little while, but when
they come on back to the corral the pony was
wet with sweat. Jake wooled him around some
more, a-makin' him turn this way an' that, then
finally he got down an' turned him loose.

"No use ridin' a young horse plumb to death,"
he says. "This pony is learnin' fast."

Jake rode ten head that day. A few of them
he forefooted. But after they had had their buck
they settled down. He pulled them around this
way an' that, a-learnin' them to rein. One little
black had gentled down so fast that after Jake

uncocked him an' wooled him around awhile he
let me get up on him an' ride him down the
wash.

It give me the queerest feelin' just settin' on
his back. I was afraid he might explode at any
time. An' still I sort of hoped he would. For I
knowed I'd have to learn sometime an' I might
as well start now. An' then again I figgered it
was just as well he didn't buck. For I knowed if
he hung his head with me an' pitched like he had
when Jake had topped him off he was bound to
spill the pack.

Jake finally turned all the ponies out except
the little black. He kept him up to wrangle on,
an' after he turned him in a little trap we went in
an' eat again.

After we got the dishes washed Jake showed
me how to tie a hondoo in a rope an' build a horn
loop too. An' when I left the ranch an' headed
West again, he give me the rope to take.

A bronc rider was my idea of a king. 'An'
Jake never made a move in them three days that
I wasn't right at his heels. But to hear Jake talk
he didn't think so much of it himself.

"There's nothin' in it, kid," he says. "For
I've been ridin' the rough string an' snappin'
broncs ever since I was old enough to make a
hand. An' all I've got to show for it is a lot of

broken bones. I'm goin' on thirty now. In any
other game a man at thirty ain't so old. But any
man who breaks horses after he's thirty is an old
man at this game."

Any man at thirty was an old man as far as I
could see, no matter what he done. You're apt
to miss a lot of things that people says when
you're goin' on fifteen.

"I'm goin' to be a bronc rider," I says. "I'd
rather do that than own a ranch."

"I reckon you'll be one then," Jake says. "I
felt that way myself. An' I was just your age
when I run away from home."

CHAPTER V

Driftin'

JAKE told me how to get to the next ranch west of there. It was nearly thirty miles an' I made it easy in a day. But I didn't land a job, nor at the next place, nor the next. I finally lost all track of time. It seemed to me I'd been away from home for years. I knowed it was six hundred miles from where we lived to Charlie's uncle's place. But how many miles I'd gone since then I didn't know. Nor how many outfits that I tried to land a job. For the ranches all looked pretty much the same to me. At most every place I stopped they always told me the same old thing: "If you had only come a few days earlier we might have put you on." I was always welcome to stop an' rest my pony up, but I couldn't land a job.

Sometime I'd miss a place that I was headed for, an' I'd have to lay out at night. I'd pull the saddle off of White Man an' turn him loose. Then I'd curl up in my saddle-blankets an' sleep

till I froze out. At first I didn't mind it none.
For I liked them great big flats. An' then blue
peaks in the distance that looked so close, yet
was always so far away. Some nights the stars
hung down so low it seems I could pick them off.
But summer soon slipped away, an' them fall
nights got mighty cold.

I've often wondered how White Man stood
up. He got tender-footed some. But he was
always fat. When I laid out I'd pull the saddle
off an' turn him loose. But he was always in
sight when it broke light. There was plenty of
coyotes now. Some nights they would yelp
awhile then quiet down, an' I wouldn't hear them
again until just before it started breakin' light.
Then they'd all cut loose an' howl. That was
always a welcome sound to me, for if the night
was cold the chances are good I'd be up a-walkin'
around by then, a-tryin' to keep warm. An'
when they all cut loose at once, I knowed that
day was comin' on.

At times I'd stay a few days at a ranch an'
rest my pony up; then hit the trail again. The
punchers teased me some, but I got so I never
minded that. An' every little while I'd happen
onto one that I liked, like Steve an' Jake. An'
there was only one place I struck, in all them

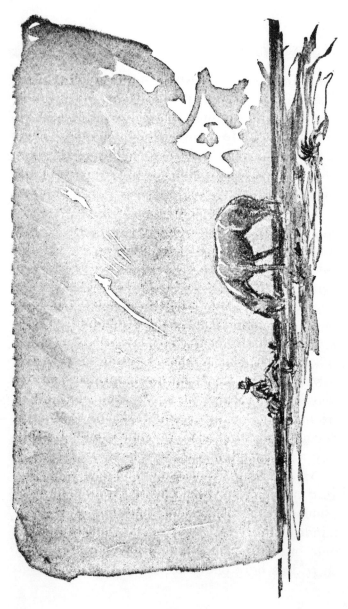

months that I was out, where they wouldn't take me in.

I'd rode most forty miles that day, an' White Man was pretty tired. I hadn't had nothin' to eat since daylight an' nothin' to drink since noon. An' when I caught sight of a windmill late that evenin' it looked mighty good to me. I rode into the water corral an' let White Man drink his fill, an' I was just ready to water out myself, when some hombre came out of the house. It never occurred to me but what he'd tell me to turn White Man loose an' come on in an' eat. But instead of that, he says he's got sickness in the house an' can't take nobody in.

"There's another ranch down the road a piece," he says. I asked him how far it was. "Not far," he says, so I didn't say no more. But it was all so strange to me I didn't quite get the thing at first. But I remember I crawled on White Man without takin' a drink. An' the sun was just a-goin' down as I rode out of the gate.

It was along in the middle of November, an' the nights was pretty cold. It was dark before I'd gone a half. But I figgered from what he said it would be only a piece down the road. I rode for two hours, mebbe, an' I never could find the place. I finally decided I'd missed it, so I

decided to lay out. But I was pretty thirsty, so
I kept a-goin' on. But I finally figgered I'd better stop before White Man quit on me.

I pulled the saddle off of White Man, an'
after I turned him loose I tried to rustle somethin' to build a fire. But there was no moon, an'
I didn't make much of a job of it. So I finally
rolled up in my saddle-blankets an' tried to get
some sleep. My clothes had wore out long ago,
an' for some time I'd been wearin' cast-off
clothes that punchers had staked me to. An' if it
hadn't been for a coat a puncher named Bill Jor-
dan had give' me I think I'd of froze that night.
It was a duckin' coat, but it was lined with wool
inside. Bill was all of six feet tall, an' the coat
was pretty much the worse for wear but it looked
good to me.

I guess I dozed off some. An' I forgot I was
thirsty, just tryin' to keep warm. For I was up
an' down a hundred times that night. I'd get
up an' run around till I was circulatin' good;
then I'd try to sleep again. But by the time the
Mornin' Star come up I was walkin' to keep
warm.

I saddled White Man up as soon as it
started breakin' light. As soon as the sun got
up, it thawed me out, but my thirst come back

again. An' as far as I could see there wasn't a
house in sight. It wasn't till about four that
evenin' that I finally come to a ranch.

A small rancher an' his wife, named Hale, was
livin' there alone. I guess I looked sort of
peaked, for as soon as I rode up he says, "Go on
in, kid, an' I'll unsaddle your horse."

Mrs. Hale was cookin' supper an' she was
makin' some kind of soup. An' to have seen the
way she acted a person might have thought that
she expected me. For she sat me down an', fillin'
up a great big bowl of soup, she sort of smiled
at me. I'd finished it an' started on another one
when Hale come into the house.

"Where'd you stay last night?" he says. I
told him I laid out, for I must have missed this
other ranch the hombre told me of. But when
I said this hombre wouldn't take me in because
of sickness in the house Hale's face got awful
hard.

"That ——— ——— ———," he says, "has
pulled that stunt before. You're not the first
boy he's turned away an' started down the road
at night. This is the place he was speakin' of,
for there is no ranch in between."

His wife never paid no hed to the fact he
swore. "Pore boy," was all she said.

But by the time I finished with the soup I was
feelin' good again. An' when they set down to
supper I was ready to eat some more. Hale's
place seemed more like home than any one I'd
struck. A low two-roomed shack made out of
boards was all it was. A table an' a few rawhide-
bottom chairs an' two beds made up the furni-
ture. But there were curtains in the windows,
an' the place was neat an' clean, an' at both windows she had flowers that she watered every day.

I stayed a week with them. Some days I rode
with Hale an' I'd have liked to have gone to
work for him. His hair was white as snow, an'
his face looked hard until he laughed, but he had
a great big boomin' voice. An' he always smiled
when he come inside the house. Hale swore
more than anyone I ever seen. But it wasn't because he was mad, and he swore inside the house
the same as he did outside. It was funny to me
at first, but his wife didn't seem to mind. An'
the minute he stuck his head inside the door she
had a smile for him.

Mrs. Hale never talked unless there was somethin' she had to say. She had a way of hummin'
when she worked, and she bustled around all
day. But there was a million wrinkles in her
face, an' her eyes looked awful tired.

She had a bunch of chickens, an' I helped her feed them things. An' each mornin' an' night I helped her milk. We only took some from each cow. We let the calves suck first an' then we took the rest. She asked me all about my folks, an' asked me wouldn't I like to go back home.

But I says not until I got a job. For I was goin' to be a cow-puncher no matter what else come.

She didn't even smile at that. Then she says she never had any girls, but she had two boys, an' they both worked away from home. For they didn't own many cattle, an' Hale looked after them.

"My boys is cowboys, too," she says. "They couldn't be nothin' else, for that's all Hale ever done." But when I asked her if they was workin' at any of the outfits near, she shook her head.

"Will is a-breakin' horses in Arizona. We hear from him sometimes. An' Tom was workin' for an outfit in Old Mexico the last we heard from him."

They urged me to stay on, an' the day I left, Hale an' his wife come out to the corral with me while I saddled White Man up. She packed a lunch for me as big as mother had, an' Hale give me a slicker that he said he never used. I

tied it on behind an' put on my duckin' coat. An'
Hale an' his wife both wished me luck as I
started down the road.

My coat had been hangin' behind the stove
ever since I struck Hale's place. An' the only
reason I put it on when I pulled out was because
the day was raw.

I reckon I rode an hour or so, for their place
was out of sight. An' there wasn't no reason
for me a-puttin' my hand in the pocket of my
coat, for there hadn't been nothin' inside of it
since I owned the thing.

I wondered what it could be at first. But
when I drawed it out, it was some nickels an'
dimes an' quarters tied up in a handkerchief.
Three dollars an' eighty-five cents it was, for I
counted it several times. It was the first money
I'd seen in weeks, an' it looked like a fortune to
me. There's no tellin' what it meant to her. For
I knowed from the way they lived that money
was mighty scarce. She had knowed well
enough I wouldn't take it if she offered it to me.
So she slipped the handkerchief inside my coat
before I started off. I sat there on my horse for
quite a spell. But I never did get to thank her,
for I never saw them again.

It begun a-drizzlin' rain along about noon.

But I was settin' pretty with a slicker now. An'
the lunch his wife had packed. An' that evenin'
just at dark I come to another ranch.

It was a big spread from the looks of it, an' the
punchers was all inside the house, for the wagon
had just come in. I stayed all night, an' next
mornin' when I left a puncher they called Tex
come on along with me. For the fall work was
over now an' they was layin' off some of the
hands. Tex had been workin' there since early
May, an' he was grass-bellied with spot cash.

"No town for me this time," says Tex. "I'm
huntin' a winter job. Last fall I blowed in eight
months' wages in a week. An' I shore had a
time. But I rode the chuck-line from then till
spring before I got another job. No town this
time for me."

Tex must have been all of twenty-five, an' that
seemed old to me. In one way he made me think
of Red. For Tex was a redhead too. But Tex
never teased me much, an' I liked to ride with
him. He was full of stories an' he laughed at
everythin'.

"No town for me this time," he'd say. "I'm
through a-passin' out my dough to the first
woman that I strike an' then a-ridin' out of town
as soon as I go broke with nothin' but a head.

Last time it even hurt to touch my hair." Tex
would laugh again. "No town for me this time."

I rode with Tex for several weeks, but we
didn't land a job. Finally the week before
Christmas we rode into a ranch, an' they was
mighty proud we'd come. Four punchers was a-
stayin' there, an' they had finally decided to cut
the cards to see which one stayed at the ranch an'
fed the ponies grain while the rest went into
town. As soon as Tex said we'd stay they got
ready to pull out. I figgered it would be nice to
stay with Tex, for I liked to be with him. But
them punchers gettin' ready to pull out was more
than he could stand. He never said a word to
me, but next mornin' when they caught their
horses up, Tex caught his too an' rode off to
town with them.

It was the first Christmas I'd ever been away
from home an' it rained all through the week.
But Christmas Eve it got colder an' started in
to snow. There was nothin' for me to do but
chunk the fire, an' the only work I had to do was
to feed the ponies grain. Each mornin' an'
evenin' when they come up I'd hang the nose-
bags on them. As soon as they finished eatin' I
pulled them off again. They told me to feed my
pony too, an' I come near founderin' him. For

White Man wasn't used to grain, but he shore
did get his fill.

The ranch looked like a boar's nest, an' I
mucked the whole place out. But the time hung
heavy on my hands, so I mucked the place each
day. I'd seen punchers cook a lot by now an' I'd
tried to help at times. But this was the first time
I ever tried to cook myself. I got along all right
a-cookin' steak, an' I could cook frijole beans all
right. But when it come to biscuits I didn't do
so well. There was several old magazines about
the place an' I wooled a heap with them. An'
there was one book I found I liked a lot, an' I
read the thing plumb through.

"Oklahoma Charlie" was the name of it. I've
often wondered who wrote the book, for I've
never seen one since. Charlie had been around a
lot an' did most everything. He was s'posed to
be a cowboy, but from what I got of it he spent
most of his time with women an' shootin' people
up.

The rain kept me inside most all the time an'
when it started in to snow on Christmas Eve I
was feelin' pretty low. For I knowed the kids
at home would hang their stockings up about
now, an' dad and mother would be lookin' wise.
I didn't believe in Santa Claus no more, but it

would be nice to be at home. So I read some more of "Oklahoma Charlie" to keep my spirits up. An' just before I went to bed I went outside to have a look around, an' the ground was white with snow.

It quit snowin' before mornin' but everythin' was white. An' the ponies was a bedraggled lot when they come in to get their grain. But as soon as I got the fire a-goin' it was warm inside the house. The snow didn't stay on long that day. For as soon as the sun come out it melted off, except where the ground was shaded by some post, an' on the north side of the house.

The ranch looked pretty clean to me. But as soon as I cooked breakfast an' got the dishes washed an' wiped I mucked the place out again. I figgered I'd take a little ride that day. For the ponies just stood around the corral an' let the sun shine on their backs. But towards noon it clouded up again an' started in to rain. An' that evenin' when I hung the nose-bags on it begun to snow again. Each mornin' when I took the nose-bags off, the ponies might stand around awhile, but finally they always went off to graze. An' they wouldn't show up until that evenin' when it was time for their grain. But for some reason or other on Christmas they stayed in the corral all day. To me that was the longest day I ever spent, an' that evenin' I swept out the place again before I went to bed.

It was the day after New Year's by the calendar, an' I was still alone. But late that evenin' I heard a yell, an' the punchers come ridin' in. It was the longest I'd ever gone before without havin' someone around. An' when I heard them squall I left the steak burn an' run outside to watch them all unsaddle.

"Hello, kid," they all says.

An' then I says, "Where's Tex?"

"Oh, him!" says one. "Last thing I seen of Tex he was drunker than seven hundred dollars an' a-walkin' off with a Mexican gal." An' then the whole bunch laughed.

"He sent you somethin', though," the puncher says. An' when the whole bunch grinned I figgered that they was kiddin' me. But the puncher untied a package he carried behind his saddle. I never had no idea what it was. An' I never had no idea what Tex might send to me. But when I got inside the house an' opened it there was a bran'-new pair of boots.

It wasn't but a second till I had my hob-nails off an' had slid inside of them, an' as I walked around the ranch-house in them high heels there

was no one livin' I'd have traded places with
right then. But that was only half of it. For
each puncher had brought me somethin'. They
give me one package at a time. An' the last
thing one of them brought in was a bran'-new
Stetson hat. I've never had a Christmas quite
like that before or since. There was a bran'-new
suit of Levi's (copper-riveted overalls without
bibs); a duckin' coat all lined with wool inside; a
suit of heavy underwear; some socks an' a flannel
shirt.

"Tex bought the boots first thing when we hit
town," says one, "before he started gettin' drunk.
Boy! he's a wampus, what I mean. An' fight!
It took all four of us to handle him when they
tried to throw him in."

"An' women!" says another. "Boy! that redhead's there."

CHAPTER VI

A Job at McDougal's

McDOUGAL'S place was down on the Arizona line. I rode in there one day at noon, still huntin' for a job. I didn't think there was an outfit in all New Mexico I'd missed. For I doubled an' circled every time I heard of a ranch. Then some puncher spoke of McDougal's, so I asked him where it was.

"No use a-goin' there," he says, "for it's a straight horse outfit. An' unless a man's a bronc-peeler he's got no chance for a job."

I had begun to wonder at times now if I ever would find work. But I figgered I'd hit McDougal's, for I might as well try them all. Anyway, thinks I, my luck can't be no worse with an outfit that raises horses than the ones that raises cows.

There was plenty of times when I thought of the folks an' the little farm back home. But it

never occurred to me to go on back. For I had
finally found the things I had wanted all my life.
An' there was only one thing in my mind an'
that was to land a job.

It was one day 'long in February when I
finally come to the ranch. As I got close enough
to make out the buildings I saw a bunch of horses
tied out around the flat. I couldn't figger it out
at first, but as I kept a-ridin' closer I saw that
they was broncs—each one with a, long rope tied
to the hackamore, so's he could move around a
lot. As I rode past one big black that was closer
than the rest, he set back an' started fightin' the
rope till he finally throwed himself. He was up
again in a jiffy a-fightin' at the rope. An', man,
what a horse he was! As I set there on little
old White Man an' watched the big black fight,
it all come over me at once that I'd never been
on a real horse. The big black must have
throwed himself a half a dozen times. An' as I
rode up to the big corrals he was still fightin' at
the rope.

There was dust a-comin' from one of the
smaller corrals, so I headed for that place. I slid
off White Man's back an' dropped the reins.
An' peekin' through the cedar poles I saw a
long lean puncher a-workin' with a bronc. The

bronc was already saddled, but he was tied down
on the ground, so I crawled up on the top of the
bars to get a better look.

The puncher never paid no hed to me, for he
was busy with the horse. He pulled the hackamore reins up short, an' gettin' as much of the
saddle under him as he could while the horse was
down, he took the foot-rope off.

The bronc didn't know that he was loose at
first. But he wasn't long in findin' out. An'
when he did he come to his feet with the puncher
in the saddle. He stood there for a second, an'
the puncher set himself. He pulled the hackamore reins up just short enough. An' as he
shoved his feet just far enough ahead to meet
the first jolt, the old bronc hung his head.

The bronc was a good-lookin' horse, as big as
the black that I just passed. He didn't beller
none when he bucked, but he was stout; every
time he hit the ground I could hear the leathers
pop. The puncher was ridin' pretty, but he
wasn't scratchin' none. He finally caught a
glimpse of me a-settin' on the rail an' flashed a
grin, but he never spoke until they'd had it out.
Finally the bronc throwed up his head. An'
after he trotted around the corral a time or two,
the puncher reached down an' caught the ear.

Next thing he was on the ground. It was all
one motion, an' done so quick I could hardly
foller him. An' it never surprised me none at all
that the bronc didn't even move.

"Hello there, kid," he says. "Turn your horse
loose. As soon as I put this bronc in another
corral we'll see what we can find to eat."

I pulled the saddle off of White Man an' follered him inside, an' when we got inside the house
there was another puncher there. The tall
puncher called him Joe, an' he was curly-haired
an' short. He was hobblin' around on sticks,
with his foot in a plaster cast. He nodded to me
when we come in. The dinner was already on
the table, so the three of us set down.

The tall puncher's name was Mack. Neither
of them paid any hed to me until we had finished eatin', but I was curious about Joe's leg,
so I asked him how it happened.

"Horse fell on me," was all he said.

But details was what I wanted, so I asked him
how that come. He looked at me an' sort of
half-way smiled.

"I ain't real shore," he says, "but I think he
wanted to."

I never said no more to that, an' finally Mack
turned to me an' says, "Lookin' for a job?"

I told him I was huntin' work but I hadn't had no luck so far.

"How would you like to go to work right here?"

"You're kiddin' now," I says. For McDougal's was the last place in the world I dreamed of ketchin' on.

"I'll tell you, kid, the old man will be in tonight, an' if you hit him for a job I think he'll put you on. We've had kids here at different times, but they all get pretty sorry when they've been around awhile. They'd be all right at first, but first thing you knowed they was throwin' off, an' there was nothin' else for the old man to do but send them down the road again."

"I won't throw off," I says, "an' I'll do anythin'." An' if there was ever anybody meant just what they said it was me a-speakin' then.

"They all say that at first," Mack says, "but the old man ain't here much. But there's plenty to do around here besides waitin' on all of us. For we stay here all the time, an' we keep two milk cows up, an' there's the old man's bunch of chickens. You'll have to feed them things."

"I can milk," I says, "an' the whole thing suits me fine."

"Mebbe it won't," Mack says, "when you've

been here a little while. For everybody is your boss an' any time a puncher shoots a pill you're s'posed to jump right through the loop."

"When will the old man be in?"

"Some time tonight," Mack says, "an' I think you can figger on the job, for he's lookin' for a kid."

I couldn't believe it myself at first, an' I was still afraid McDougal might have other plans. But just the same I started in to work right then, for it helped to let off steam.

I was for washin' the dishes as soon as Mack went back to the corral. But Joe says there's two more punchers due in any time an' to let the dishes wait. But I couldn't any more set around right then than I could fly. So I grabbed the broom an' started to muck the kitchen out. But Joe put a stop to that. The dust was pretty thick. But I guess he knowed just how I felt, for finally he laughed an' says: "If you're dead set on startin' in right now, go into the other room."

The place may have been cleaned by others who did a better job. But I'm bettin' it was never cleaned by anyone who put on more real speed. It was another long, low-roofed affair with three or four separate rooms. I knew the

one in the end was McDougal's, for there was a
great big desk in there, an' there was pictures of
horses all around the walls. I'd liked to have
stopped an' looked at them. But I figgered
there'd be another time for that. An' the only
time I stopped was occasionally to poke my head
outside for air—an' let the broom cool off a bit.
For I was workin' in a fog, an' I kept the old
broom hot.

I finally got the place mucked out, an' as I sort
of staggered out the door I heard an old familiar
laugh an' someone squalled at me: "Hello there,
Button. What you doin' here?"

It was Tex, an' when he said he was workin'
here it seemed to me that everythin' had finally
started breakin' right for me. An' it had started
all at once. It never had occurred to me that
I'd ever see him again an' get to thank him for
the boots.

"I'm much obliged," I says, "an' they shore
fit me fine."

"Never mind about the boots," he says.
"Come on outside an' let's have a look at you.
You're lookin' fine, but you ain't growed a bit
as far as I can see."

"Mebbe I'm goin' to get a job," I says, "when
the old man comes in tonight."

"Don't you worry about the job," he says, "for he's been lookin' for a kid ever since I landed here. I never had any idea where you was or I'd have sent for you."

But in spite of all Tex had to say I couldn't be real shore. An' as I waited for the old man to come I'd get full of panic at the thought of it. I even pictured him drivin' in with a wagonful of kids.

Tex said he'd got drunk again an' blowed all his money in. But he had happened onto Mack in town. Mack was lookin' for a peeler, so he come on out with him.

"Thought you wasn't goin' to town," I says, "an' let no woman get your dough."

An' then Tex laughed again. "I always say that, Button, but I always slip again. An' I shore had a time this trip. The woman was a Mexican, an' say—"

The outfit didn't have a cook, an' everybody worked. That night at supper Mack cooked the bread, an' Tex the meat; an' Joe an' I peeled the spuds. The other puncher's name was Dave an' he didn't come in till late. Mack helped me feed the chickens, an' we was both down in the corral a-milkin' when McDougal come drivin' in. My heart skipped several beats when he drove in with that big four-horse team. But things looked pretty good, I thought, for he was by himself.

I was for quittin' my cow right then an' not wastin' any time. But Mack laughed an' says I'd better finish milkin' first, for the old man wouldn't run off.

It was nearly dark, an' he looked awful tall as he got down off the seat. "Just let the wagon stand," he says, "an' we'll unload in the mornin'." But he helped unhook the horses before he went inside the house.

The old man was sittin' at the table when

Mack an' I come in. He nodded to Mack an'
looked at me an' says, "Hello there, bub."

Now was my time, I thought, but I couldn't
say a word. So I finally bobbed my head at him,
an' helped Mack strain the milk. We set the big
pans on a table that stood outside the door. An'
while we was scaldin' the strainer an' the buckets
out the old man left the table.

I'd lost my chance, I figgered, when he went
into the other room. But Mack says as long as
I'm squirmin' so he'll speak to him right now.

I waited an age, it seemed to me, an' I'd begun
to think most anythin' when Mack yells, "Come
in here, kid."

Mack was settin' on his heels a-smokin' a cigarette. But McDougal was settin' at his desk.
When I come in, the old man looked at me an'
pulled that white mustache of his an' that little
jigger underneath for quite a spell before he
finally spoke.

"Mack says you want to work."

"I do," I says, "an' I'll do anythin'."

"Shore you didn't run away from home?" he
says, a-lookin' at me real close.

I told him I had run off one other trip, but this
trip dad let me go; an' I told him just what dad
had said that day when I left home.

That seemed to satisfy the old man, for after he took dad's name, he says, "I'll pay you fifteen dollars a month an' see how you make out."

An' then he told me the same thing Mack had said earlier in the day about everyone a-bossin' me, an' about the cows to milk. But if he had told me I had to jump off the windmill tower twice a day I'd have agreed to it. "That's all," he finally says, but as I was walkin' out the door he called to me again. "Another thing," he says, "Stay off these bad horses, or the boys will get you killed."

"How did you come out?" Tex says. But he knowed well enough by lookin' at my face that I had got a job. Tex an' Joe both seemed to take the thing for granted, for they never said no more.

I walked outside so's I could be alone, for I was afraid I'd make a fool of myself in front of Tex an' Joe.

Anyone to have seen my tracks that night would have thought that I was drunk, an' I spent the next hour just talkin' to myself. Fifteen dollars a month seemed like all the money in the world to me. For in them days in New Mexico old hands like Mack an' Tex was only gettin' thirty.

The moon had just come up, an' I finally spied White Man off a ways, a-grazin' on the flat. So I headed out towards him. I always talked to him when us two was alone, an' in the last few months White Man had heard everything that was ever on my mind. Little old White Man raised his head an' looked at me when I come walkin' up.

"Well, White Man," I says, a-rarin' back an' tryin' to look as big as possible, "I've finally got a job."

CHAPTER VII

"All Set?"

THE old man was seldom at the ranch except for a few days at a time. Mack was the boss when he was gone, but everyone bossed me. Each mornin' we rolled out with the mornin' star, an' we worked seven days a week. While the punchers was cookin' breakfast I fed the chickens an' milked my two old cows. I kept both calves penned up, an' in the mornin' both cows would be waitin' just outside, when I showed up with my pails. I turned the old cows in with them; an' after the calves had sucked awhile I cut them in another corral until I finished milkin'. By the time I got back to the house an' got the milk all strained an' had scalded the buckets an' the strainer out, breakfast was usually ready.

Mack mostly made the bread, for he was the best bread-cook, an' Tex usually fried the meat.

87

It was hung out each night, an' in the mornin' they wrapped it in a big meat tarp an' put it in the shade. Most everyone did somethin', an' while the meal was cookin' they all set around the kitchen on their heels a-playin' the coffee-pot an' smokin' cigarettes. The meals never varied much. We had steak an' eggs or salt pork for breakfast, hot bakin'-powder biscuits, frijole beans an' lick. Sometimes we had potatoes, an' there was always some kind of fruit—mostly dried peaches or apricots, for the outfit was burnt out on prunes.

I usually put on the pot of fruit to cook when the outfit had finished breakfast. I never minded to cook the fruit, for that didn't take so long; but frijole beans had to cook for hours before they was fit to eat, an' I was forever forgettin' them. Mebbe someone would be ready to top off a bronc, an' I'd be down in the corral a-waitin' to see the fun; an' just before they took the foot-rope off, it was usually my luck to have some-one say, "How's them beans a-comin' on?" That was my cue to make a high lope for the house. An' often the beans would be boiled dry, an' the fire out by the time I looked at them.

Long about ten o'clock some puncher would put on the roast or mebbe a mess of ribs, an' for

dinner we'd have ribs or roast, hot biscuits, frijole beans an' lick, an' we'd have fruit again. At
night we varied it with steak an' mebbe canned
corn, but no matter what else we cooked we always had hot biscuits, frijole beans, an' lick.

There was always wood to cut, an' I usually
mucked the place out each day. But if the
peelers was workin' in the corral it never took
me long. For every minute I was free I spent
down in the corrals. When I was down there
it was always, "Hey, kid, open that outer gate,"
or, "Button, bring me another rope, while I tie
this damn bronc down."

I had been at the ranch most two weeks I
guess, an' one mornin' I was helpin' Mack. He
had just topped off a little gray that was smaller
than the rest. He finally got holt of an ear, an'
as he stepped down to the ground he looked at
me an' says, "Want to try him, kid?"

It was just what I'd been waitin' for, an' the
minute I bobbed my head, Mack eared the little
gray horse down an' told me to pile on. Mack
was all of six feet tall, an' I couldn't reach the
stirrups by a foot, but I pulled up the hackamore
reins until I figgered it was right.

"Don't take too short a holt," says Mack, "or
he'll jerk it right away from you the minute he

bogs his head. All set?" I nodded that I was
an' Mack turned the gray horse loose.

One jump, I think, was all he made, but it was
all so quick I couldn't hardly tell. For the next
thing I knowed I was on the ground with both
hands full of dirt. But it hadn't hurt me none,
an' as soon as Mack eared the little gray down
again I made another try. This one was just
as short an' sweet as the first fall that I made,
and this time it dazed me some, so I wasn't near
so keen; but Mack eared him down an' I got on.

"Never mind the hackamore this time," he
says. "Jest get a holt of that old horn an' screw
down on it. All set?" I nodded that I was an'
Mack turned him loose.

This time I done real good or at least I
thought I was, for by pullin' all the leather off
the saddle-horn I rode the gray four jumps, an'
I'd begun to think that I might stick. When
all at once one of the stirrups caught me over my
right eye an' knocked me loose again. Next
jump my shirt caught on the saddle-horn an'
tore the thing plumb off.

I must have set there on the ground for quite
a spell, for Mack had the gray horse caught. I
was sort of wobbly on my pins, but when I tried
to get back on, Mack said I'd had enough.

"Ain't hurt none, kid?" 'An' when I shook my head he laughed. I watched Mack get up on the little gray, an' there's no denyin' I was feelin' low. It wasn't because of my right eye, though it was swellin' shut; it was because I'd finally got a chance at the thing I wanted all my life, an' I'd messed the whole thing up.

Mack finally turned the little gray outside, an' as he come on back to me, "That eye's a pip," he says.

"Do you think I'll ever learn to ride?" I says.

"You're dog-gone right," says Mack. "Jest keep a-tryin' like you done today, an' you'll soon be snappin' broncs. For that's the way we all begin." Then I felt good again.

As soon as the peelers finished snappin' out a bunch of broncs they brought a new bunch in. The ones they'd broke was either turned back out or McDougal sold them off. I had two horses in my mount, Dodger an' Old Blake. An' when the peelers left to gather another bunch of horses I usually went along.

McDougal seldom broke a colt that was under four years old. An' in every bunch we hazed in, there was some that was eight or ten. They all run back in the lower hills, an' most of them was wild. For they was never handled any, from

the time they was branded until we got them up to break.

The peelers all went whenever we left to bring a new bunch in. We'd circle a bunch we wanted an' head them towards the ranch. An' the races we had from there to the ranch would satisfy any kid. Sometimes we'd have a bunch all headed right an' everything was fine, when some owl-headed bronc up in the lead would decide on some place else. There was some broncs Mc-Dougal owned that we never did get penned; an' how many horses McDougal had, he didn't know himself.

As soon as we got a bunch of new ones penned there was always the stock horses—mares an' colts—to cut out that had come on in with them. Then each bronc was roped, an' after he choked down, a hackamore was put on his head. Then he was tied outside with a long rope, so's he could move around a lot. An' most of them, after they'd fought the ropes an' throwed themselves a time or so, would begin to quiet down. Specially, as soon as their noses got sore from pullin' on the ropes.

I've seen Mack spend an hour just foolin' with a bronc. He would tie one hind foot. An' put the blanket on an' pull it off, an' rub the old pony with it, until the bronc finally got it through his head he wasn't goin' to be hurt. Then he'd put the saddle on an' pull it off, till the bronc got used to it. Then first thing the old bronc knew, Mack had took the foot-ropes off an' was sittin' on his back. Most of them pitched at first. But Mack never spurred or whipped a horse unless he needed it. Most horses is mighty quick to learn if a man knows how to handle them, an' any time you see a horse that's spoilt you can usually trace it back to some

puncher that has rode him. Whenever Mack got
through with one it wasn't a one-man horse.

It's as natural for a bronc to fight an' pitch
at first, as it is for a duck to swim. That's the
only weapon a pony has, an' he's only tryin' to
protect himself, for at first he's scared to death.
Of course, there's always some you can't be easy
on. An' they whip it out of them. Then again
you'll find a bronc that will never give up, an' the
more a puncher fights him the more he fights
back. For horses is just like humans, an' each
of them has different ways. An' there's a heap
of difference between breakin' one and ridin' in a
contest. Some people who can ride most anythin' ain't fit to break a horse. An' on a ranch,
whenever you find a peeler that's rough, he's
always given horses that fight him back an' play
the same game he does.

Around a horse outfit where they're snappin'
broncs there's always some man hurt. Some
peelers is just unlucky. Joe had the same leg
broke three times while I was workin' there; an'
Tex was laid up a half-dozen times—while Mack
was never hurt.

The peelers kidded me a lot about that eye of
mine. But it wasn't long before I learned to
ride. For as soon as the punchers let the ham-

mer down on some new bronc, they'd let me try
him out. At first they picked out ones that
didn't pitch so hard, an' as I kept doin' better
they give me tougher ones. I couldn't reach
none of their stirrups by a foot. An' I got
plenty of falls. "Want to try this one, kid?"
they'd say, an' any time McDougal wasn't anywheres around I'd crawl up in the saddle. I was
mighty lucky too. For there's hardly a day I
wasn't on some buckin' horse. An' besides a long
cut over my right eye, a broken nose was all I
had to show for the first six months I rode.

I'd been there most six months I guess, an' I
was pretty cocky. I'd tried every horse they'd
let me on, an' I hadn't been bucked off in most
two weeks, when they caught up a little black
an' told me I could ride him.

"You can use your own saddle too," Mack
says. "An' instead of toppin' him off in one
of the smaller corrals you can ride him in the
big one."

That suited me, an' Mack held the black while
I laced my saddle on. Joe an' Tex both stood
around with some blankets in their hands. Mack
eared the black horse down an' waited till I got
all set.

"Let's see a real ride this time," says Tex.

"Take your hat off an' start right in on him
first jump. All set?" Mack says.

I said I was an' Mack turned the pony loose.
Tex an' Joe both throwed their blankets under
him so I didn't get to fan. For the old bronc
made about four jumps that was so high an' wide
it was all I could do to keep my seat. I was
pullin' leather by the time we went into the fence,
an' the old bronc hit that fence on high. Next
thing I knowed I was layin' in the shade an' the
boys was workin' over me. But the minute I set
up an' looked around Mack says, "Mebbe, your
hat will fit you now." An' then the whole bunch
laughed.

My nose felt pretty sore for several days, an'
both my eyes was black. But Mack was right
about my hat, for I was fairly quiet for a spell.
I was afraid if McDougal should happen in he
would fire me then an' there, for he had told me
several times to keep off them bad horses. Mc-
Dougal had wrote to dad an' told him where I
was. An' dad had wrote back an' said I hadn't
run away. I imagine McDougal had some idea
of what was goin' on, for several times he said
to me:

"Stay off them broncs, Button, for you're a
long ways from home."

We hadn't seen the old man for a month when one night he come a-drivin' in. Tex an' Joe was laid up right then, an' I was in the room with them. It was after supper an' Mack an' the old man was talkin' in his room. Finally I heard the old man say to Mack that if some light rider come along to put him on, for he wanted some young colts broke. An' then I most quit breathin', for I heard Mack say, "Why don't you put Button on?"

"They'd kill that kid," the old man says. "He don't know how to ride."

"The deuce he don't," says Mack. "He's been ridin' for six months, an' ridin' tough horses too."

The old man never said no more to that, an' I eased outside the house. I had to let off steam some way, an' I thought the thing was fixed. For while I was down a-talkin' to White Man on the flat I saw his light go out.

Next mornin' the old man never had a word to say, in spite of the fact that I took plenty of pains to let him know that I was there. For I was busier than a coon dog all about the place, an' I swept the whole place out before it started breakin' light—except the room where Tex an' Joe was, an' they wouldn't stand for that.

It was while I was feedin' the chickens that

the old man spoke to me. An' when he spoke it
was like havin' cold water throwed all over me.

"Thought I told you to stay off them broncs,"
he said a-lookin' at me real hard.

"You did," I says, "but I won't do it any more
if you jest let me stay."

With that the old man grunted an' stroked his
white mustache. "I might have expected it," he
says; "but as long as you've gone an' learned to
ride, I'll tell you what I'll do. There's a bunch
of colts that I want broke. Mack will show you
the ones."

"That suits me fine," I says, an' if the old man
hadn't been a-standin' there, I'd have gone to
turnin' flips.

"Another thing," he says. "I'll raise your
wages too. I can't pay you as much as the other
boys, but I'll give you twenty a month. An' I'll
buy you another saddle, for that one of yours
is no good."

At that the old man walked inside the house
an' left me standin' there. The minute he was
gone I beat it for the corrals to tell Mack of my
good luck. Mack sort of grinned, but he was
never much on talk. Joe an' Tex was both
a-playin' pitch, an' after I told them I hunted
White Man up.

He always grazed around the ranch an' he
never did go far, an' the minute I showed up he
always raised his head as if there was somethin'
up, an' usually there was.

"White Man," I says, "you may not know it,
but I'm a-gettin' on."

CHAPTER VIII

Broncs and Peelers

McDOUGAL went to town next day, an' it was
a long old week for me. Then one night while I
was a-milkin' he come a-drivin' in. I quit my
cow the minute he come in sight. An' I was on
tap when he drove up, to help unhook the team.
'An' when we pulled off the wagon-sheet that covered all the stuff, first thing I spied was that
saddle of mine, settin' right on top.

But it wasn't until we got the load all off that
I could look it over good. Mack an' me both
looked it over then. An' then I packed it in the
house to show to Tex an' Joe. But they was
both a-playin' pitch, an' as neither of them got
excited none I packed it out again. I wouldn't
even lay it on the ground. After I'd been over it
mebbe twenty times, I put it in the rack. The

night was clear an' there hadn't been no rain in
months, but before I went to bed I hunted up a
piece of tarp an' covered it all up.

But it didn't look new for very long; it was
soon skinned up. For them colts, for all that
they was small, was mighty rough on it. Mack
cut me ten head of them, an' as soon as I got
that bunch rode out, he cut me ten head more.

It took me one whole day to get hackamores
on the first ten that I rode. Mack helped me get
them in the corral an' then he walked away.
"Them's yours," was all he says. But every
little while he'd drop around to see how I was
makin' out.

I remember the first one was a little bay. I
finally roped him round the neck, an' he must
have drug me twenty times around the corral
before I got a dally round the snubbin' post. But
once I got a dally round the post, he wasn't long
in chokin' down, an' the minute he went down
I was on his head. There was nothin' to it then.
For I wasn't long in slippin' on the hackamore,
an' once I got it on I anchored him to the fence.

The next one was a little black that dodged
an' ducked around, an' I was such a pore roper
then I like to never got him caught. But once
I got my dallies around the snubbin' post it

didn't take me long. By the time I got the last one caught an' had them all tied out, the sun was pretty low.

Mack helped me milk that night, an' it helped a lot, for my hands was all skinned up. I didn't know whether he was kiddin' me or not, an' I was too proud to care. "Since you're a-breakin' horses now," he says, "we'll split the milkin' up."

Next mornin', the first one that I rode was a little snip-nosed bay. I finally drug him into one of the smaller corrals an' after foolin' for twenty minutes I got a foot tied up. I slapped him with the blankets an' wooled with him a lot until he finally didn't seem to care, no matter what I done. But the minute I pulled up the latigo the saddle cocked way up behind.

Mack an' Tex both showed up just about that time. They did considerable coachin', but they both set on the fence. "Go right ahead," they says. "Don't pay no hed to us. Careful of that new saddle, or you'll get it all skinned up."

The little bay wasn't no bigger than White Man, but he was full of dynamite, so I finally got a loop around both front feet an' throwed him to the ground. Then, gettin' as much of the saddle under me as I could while he was down, I took the foot-rope off. An' when the little bay

come up I was settin' in the saddle. He stood
there for a second before he hung his head. Next
thing I knowed he broke into a bellerin' like a
steer. He pitched straight for the fence an'
never made no move to turn. An' when we went
into it I thought the jig was up. For Snip Nose
hit the fence head on, an' rolled plumb over me.
But he was the one that got the jar; it never
hurt me none. An' when he got to his feet again
I was settin' in the saddle.

Mack an' Tex was both on top of him the
minute he went down. For they figgered mebbe
the stirrup was smashed or I might be caught in
the riggin'. But as soon as they found that
everything was jake they crawled back on the
fence again. But the jolt the horse got when
he hit the fence was most too much for him, an'
it wasn't long after he got to his feet that Snip
Nose's head was up. He trotted around the
corral a few times, but as soon as Mack opened
the gate an' turned us out, he hung his head
again. I rode him around the flat awhile an'
pulled him around this way an' that; an' when
we finally got back to the corral an' I stepped
off, it was hard to tell who was done up the worst,
me or the snip-nose bay.

Next one I picked was one called Stripe. **He**

never pitched a lick, but he come near tearin'
up my saddle. For the minute I cinched him
up, he throwed himself, an' first thing that hit
was the saddle-horn. I'd get him on his feet
again an' think he was straightened out, when
over he'd go again right on my bran'-new saddle.
Mack an' Tex had a heap of fun about it, but it
wasn't funny to me.

"There goes the new saddle now," Tex says.
"I think I'd pull it off of him an' ride that goat
bareback."

"I'd put it on the other way," Mack says.
"Just switch the thing around. By puttin' the
cinch around his back an' lettin' the saddle hang
under his belly, you can get on easy while he's
down."

Naturally this wasn't settin' well with me, for
every time that saddle hit the dirt it was like
losin' so much blood for me. But I finally got
him straightened out, an' once I topped him he
never even humped his back with me, but trotted
off just like an old cow-horse. Stripe learned
quicker than any one I had, an' it wasn't a week
until I could crawl all over him an' turn him on
a dime.

Mack told me to take it easy or I'd work myself out of a job. But I rode five head of them

that day an' never did get throwed. That night
I tied them out again an' fed them all some hay.
But they didn't do much eatin' an' they all just
stood around. At that they didn't have anythin'
on me. Of course, I eat my supper, but while
Mack an' I was milkin' I dropped off asleep.

Them days, I think, with that first bunch of
broncs was the happiest ones I ever had. We'd
crawl out with the mornin' star. Our boot-heels
poppin' on the kitchen floor before it started
breakin' light. You could tell who each puncher
was by the jingle of his spurs. Mack had give'
me a pair of old Cross L's, that was most twice
as big as the other punchers wore. An' I must
have been a funny sight, for I was all boots an'
spurs.

As soon as the fire was started, the coffee-pot
was put on. An' while the breakfast was cookin'
we all just set around. The chairs was seldom
used, for the punchers jest squatted on their
heels while we drank that red-hot coffee, an'
smoked our cigarettes. Hot biscuits, frijole
beans an' lick, an' steak cooked in the taller.
Some of the punchers never eat any breakfast
'cept coffee an' cigarettes. But I always staggered away from the table as full as an old pot-
houn'.

I took my turn on wrangle now, an' we split
the milkin' up. An' every third mornin' I'd be
out in the corral an hour before it was light. At
McDougal's we always kept a bronc to wrangle
on; an' that always meant a show, for the pony
had been standin' out all night, an' them nights
got pretty cold. He'd always have a hump in his
back when you laced the saddle on, an' most of
them had to be throwed an' tied down before I
could get on. That hour before daylight was
always the lowest time for me, when I didn't
have no coffee in my paunch before I started out.
'After the sun gets up awhile, a horse don't look
so mean, but to hear one snort when you walk
up to him while it's still dark, especially if he's
got rollers in his nose, always sent a chill through
me. But no matter how cold the mornin' was,

by the time I'd saddled an' crawled a bronc I'd
be circulatin' good.

At first I always uncocked mine inside of the
corral. But most of them hung their heads the
minute they come out the gate. Sometimes I
could talk one out of it, by sort of easin' him real
slow. But chances are good he'd break in two
first time I struck a lope. So it was just as well
to have it out with him first thing. By the time
I got the ponies rounded up an' headed for the
ranch the chances are good the bronc had hung
his head with me a half-dozen times.

The peelers would usually be waitin' at the
corral when I showed up with the ponies, an' as
soon as I pulled the saddle off I'd grab a bite
to eat. There was never any hurry at Mc-
Dougal's, an' I liked my victuals in the mornin'.
But I never killed no time when the outfit was
at the corrals.

It was always fun to fool with some young
horse, after the sun got up; an' the different
nature each one had always interested me. Some
ponies was mighty quick to learn; but there was
always owl-heads in the bunch that you had to
haul around. An' it took a lot of strong-arm
stuff to learn them goats to rein. An' I was always ready for another bait of grub long before
twelve o'clock.

Sometimes when we was out in the hills after a
new bunch of broncs we wouldn't get in till late.
I liked them races we had so well I'd forget that
we hadn't eat for mebbe fifteen hours. But I
always made up for it when we got in that night.

The evenin's was mighty short when we was
workin'. An' everyone was satisfied to just set
around an' talk. Sometimes we all played pitch
at two bits a corner, or mebbe stud-poker at ten
cents a bean, for McDougal wouldn't stand for
no high playin'. We was usually in the hay by
nine o'clock.

Riders was always comin' an' goin' at Mc-
Dougal's. An' I soon learned to spot them by
their rigs. Most of them who come was peelers,
an' the average cow-hand only stayed all night.
For the average cowboy likes his gentle horses.
An' at a horse outfit them kind is mighty scarce.
Occasionally, we'd get a dally man who rode a
center-fire saddle. But most of the peelers who
come along wasn't packin' no rawhide rope an'
when it come to saddles they rode the double-rig.

I'd set around pop-eyed an' listen to their talk.
For some of them had rode from Canada to Old
Mexico. An' I always felt mighty small when
one of them strung out. Naturally, they all
talked horses, an' they was mighty easy to be

around. Of all the ones that ever come along
an' worked at McDougal's, there was only one
I never liked.

Mack put one on awhile we called "Pretty
Dick." But we never used the handle when he
happened to be near. He come along one night
not long after Joe an' Dave had quit, a-ridin' a
big, good-lookin' horse with lots of pretties on
his rig. But the average peeler is long on that,
so we paid no hed to it. Mack talked to him
awhile an' finally put him on. He wasn't as
good a hand as Mack or Tex, but there's no
denyin' he could ride.

At first he talked enough but not too much.
But nothin' ever quite suited him. I always got
steamed up when Mack or Tex made a real good
ride, but he always laid the heavy stone on me.

"Pretty good," he'd say, but he didn't like
some little thing in the way they handled a horse.

He had rode from Canada to Old Mexico, an'
he had a way of tellin' it as if Mack an' Tex was
hicks. He had never rode for anythin' except
the real big spreads. An' he'd tell of some outfit
where he'd worked, an' how they done, in a way
that would make me feel like we was herdin'
goats. Yep, he never just said so in as many
words, but he was doin' us all a favor by just

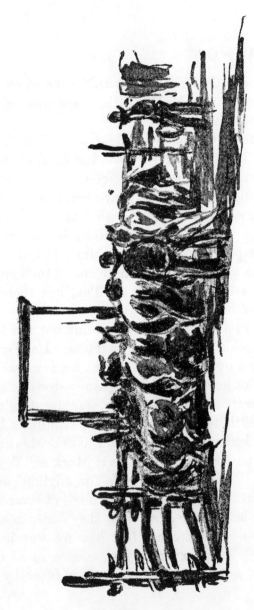

110

a-workin' here. Naturally, it all went down with
me at first.

Another thing he was always talkin' on—he
had never fixed no fence or ever worked none on
the ground. Mack an' Tex both split the milkin'
up with me, an' they'd help do everythin'. An'
most of the peelers who come along acted just
the way they did. An' there was plenty of
peelers who happened along, too, that wasn't too
proud to milk. For we wasn't peddlin' out the
stuff. An' most peelers wasn't slow to say how
good it was after usin' the stuff in cans. But
Pretty was too proud to milk.

"Chickens!" says Pretty Dick to me, an' then
he'd sort of half-way smile. "Chickens at a
ranch." As if we all was takin' pride in waitin'
on them lousy things. But Pretty never throwed
off none when it come to eatin' eggs.

The talk at night around a ranch is mostly of
the work that day. An' the horses is all rode
over plenty of times while the men is settin'
around. It was always funny to hear Tex or
Mack. They was both top hands, an' knowed
it too, but they never took themselves too serious.
There was always plenty of laughs from them
whenever they told a thing.

But Pretty Dick had a way of tellin' a thing

as if bronc ridin' started with him. He shore
was full of words all right. An' after I'd listen
for a while about some ride he made, or how he
had handled a certain horse, I'd begin to wonder
if he didn't have somethin' up his sleeve I didn't
get, although I'd seen the ride. Once I spoke
of it to Mack.

"He's good, all right," Mack says, "for after
I hear him talk awhile I begin to wonder how
we ever got along until that bird showed up."

It happened one mornin' in the corral, what
I'd been hopin' for. Pretty had crawled a big
sorrel that was too much horse for him. An' the
sorrel horse spread Pretty all over the corral.
Pretty Dick's face was white an' drawn when he
crawled back on again. I'm not belittlin' his
ridin' an' don't think he wasn't game. But the
sorrel was naturally too much horse for him an'
he busted Pretty again.

We drug him over in the shade, an' soon as he
set up Mack says if Pretty don't mind he'd try
the horse himself. Pretty looked rather peaked,
but he never said a word.

"Chances is good he'll throw me too," Mack
says. Then he winked at me an' Tex. "For I've
never been around, an' me an' Tex is just a
couple of lint-backs [cotton-pickers] that is

doin' the best we can, an' it's always been our
luck to work for some Jim 'Crow outfit instead
of the bigger spreads."

Pretty got just what he meant, for his face
turned white as chalk. Then Mack crawled up
on the sorrel without even changin' saddles.

I've seen plenty of rides since then, for that
was long ago. But I've never seen a real one
since that I don't think back to it. For the sorrel
was a big, stout horse, which would weigh twelve
hundred pounds. Pretty had screwed down in
the cinch with both his spurs, an' he'd pulled all
the leather there was in sight, an' still the sorrel
had unloaded him.

But first thing Mack done the minute he
stepped acrost was to reach way up an' hook the
sorrel in the shoulders an' hit him with his hat.
I'd never seen Mack spur a horse like that, an'
he'd often spoke to me about tearin' a pony up.
"We're not contestin'," he'd say. "We're hired
to break a horse an' learn him everything we can,
without half killin' him."

The sorrel made several jumps before he
turned on good. Every time he hit the ground
we could hear the leathers pop. But Mack still
raked him with his spurs. "Show me somethin',
sorrel horse," Mack finally yells at him. "I'm

just a pore old country boy a-tryin' to get
on."

Somethin' choked up inside of me an' I
couldn't say nothing.

"Oh, you ridin' fool!" yells Tex, an' then he
begun to cuss.

An' the sorrel horse still wiped it up, with
Mack still deep in the wood. An' every jump
the sorrel took he raked him with his spurs.

Finally the big jolts begun to slacken, an' he
didn't hit so hard. But Mack was still rakin'
him when the sorrel's head come up. The sorrel
stood there shakin' when Mack stepped off to
the ground. An' Mack was shakin' some himself, an' his face was awful white. Mack pulled
the saddle off the sorrel, an' he never said a word
until I went to turn the horse outside.

"You can have him, Button," he says then.
"He'll be a good horse for you to ride when you
drive the milk cows up."

We all went in the house an' eat, an' Mack
never said no more. Pretty was quiet too, until
Mack an' Tex had gone outside. But while I
was washin' the dishes he explained it all to me
an' just how he got throwed. The sorrel wasn't
much of a horse, he says, an' he'd rode lots
tougher ones. I didn't say much, but it wasn't

goin' down with me. An' as soon as I got the dishes washed I hunted up Mack an' Tex.

When I told them what Pretty had said, Tex started in to cuss. But Mack just laughed about it; then finally he says:

"Pride is a good thing, Button, an' I wouldn't give two bits for a man that didn't have lots of pride. But any man who lets his pride just swaller him is ridin' for a fall."

I didn't get just what Mack meant, an' I agreed with Tex when he says that Pretty Dick should be writin' stories—"he knows so dog-gone much."

CHAPTER IX

Ridin' in for Christmas

MACK shuffled the cards an' told me that I could have the first cut, an' it was a big relief to me when I turned up the jack of spades. For the thought of spendin' Christmas alone again didn't set so well with me. A new hand named Billy Moore cut next, an' when he turned up the trey of hearts he tore the blame thing up. Tex cut the nine of clubs, an' I know that he was most as relieved as me. For that redhead hadn't been to town since the Fourth of July, an' he was a-rarin' to go. Mack finally cut the five of hearts, an' Billy was elected to stay. The three of us pulled out for town next mornin' about sunup.

Mack was ridin' a gentle horse. But me an' Tex was ridin' broncs. An' the last thing Billy says when we rode off was that he hoped all

116

three of us broke our necks. I was ridin' a big
red roan; he was all horse, too. An' I admired
my shadow on the ground till Mack started kiddin' me. For me an' Tex was dolled up in our
best.

I wore a bran'-new Stetson hat, creased just
like Tex's an' Mack's. An' I wore it pulled
down over my right eye the way Tex wore his.
I had on a new pair of shop-made boots, that I
wore inside my pants. An' I was wearin' Ore-
gon breeches—the first I ever owned. Tex had
give me my first shave the night before we left,
so I had a right to be proud.

That fuzz on my face had worried me a heap.
An' several times when I was alone, I figgered
I'd sneak Mack's razor out, but I always lost my
nerve. Then the night before we left, while
Mack an' Tex was shavin', I finally spoke right
up. They made the usual remarks about smear-
in' my face with cream an' a-leavin' the cat to
lick it off. An' Mack figgered they ought to tie
me down, but they finally got it through. An'
Tex rubbed some stuff all over my face that most
set me on fire.

But that mornin' when we rode off to town
I wasn't the only shadow-rider in the bunch, for
I'd ketch Tex lookin' at his. Boy! he was feelin'

good that day; he laughed an' kidded at everything. He was wearin' a new green shirt underneath his duckin' coat.

"I'll say the women is due for a treat," Mack
says, "when you two birds hit town."

Mack was a puncher I never quite understood.
An' there was plenty of other peelers felt just
the way I did. I liked him better than anyone
I'd ever known. But when everybody else was
goin' strong, the more fun they was havin' the
quieter Mack got. He always bought his round
of drinks, but he never drank none himself. He
always took cigars instead, an' no one ever ques-
tioned it. An' no one knowed where he was
from, an' if he had any kin-folks he never mentioned them.

Clothes never bothered him at all. He dressed
just the same in town as he did back on the ranch.
He was easy to look at too, on a horse or on the
ground. An' whenever I'd look at that long
back of his I'd cuss my runty shape. I'd filled
out some since I left home, an' my shoulders was
gettin' wider, but my legs was just the same as
near as I could see! they hadn't got any longer.

It shore felt good to me to just be ridin' along.
Tex an' me did most of the talkin' now. For
after we'd rode awhile Mack never said no more.

Sometimes he'd raise his head an' flash his grin at somethin' that we said. When he did I always got a look at them white teeth of his. I never could figger out if they was as white as they really looked, or if it was just because of his dark skin. I liked to watch Mack flash that grin, for his whole face softened up, an' mostly it looked hard.

I'd been to town a time or two since I'd been at McDougal's place. Once the old man took me in with him, but we went on the wagon. Then I'd rode in with the outfit on the Fourth. But then I was ridin' White Man. Little old White Man, there'd never be another horse like him. But lots of things had happened in the last six months, an' I was most growed up. For I was breakin' horses now—an' I was goin' into town with Mack an' Tex, ridin' a big roan bronc. White Man was all right for a kid, but there wasn't no kick to ridin' him like there was a big, stout bronc.

The three of us jogged along all day, an' finally we all quit talkin'. An' I could watch my shadow all I pleased, for they paid no hed to me. That evenin' we come to the H's an' the three of us rode in an' turned our horses loose, an' went on in the house.

The H's was a cow-spread south of us, an' it was only a short day's ride from there to town. The outfit had finished supper when we come, but the cook dug up some chuck for us; an' after we downed the bait, Mack an' me washed the dishes.

That night they all had quite a game, for the H's was quite a spread. I was mostly out of it, for I could tell by the way the punchers spoke to me that they took me for just a kid. The talk run all the way from ridin' broncs an' punchin' cows to a new sheriff they all knowed. As long as they talked stock I'd set with both ears cocked, but when it got into politics I hunted up my bed, an' I'd been asleep for quite a spell, for I never heard Mack crawl in.

Next mornin' when we left for town nine punchers from the H's come along with us. They all rode gentle horses, an' I got quite a kick. For when we topped our horses off, that roan of mine was the only one that pitched. There's no denyin' I could have eased him off an' talked him out of it. But I wasn't missin' no chances with an audience like that. They might figger me for a slick-faced kid, but I'd show them I could ride. An' every time that old roan hit the ground I hit him with my hat.

As soon as we got strung out we all just jogged along. I was paired off with the cook awhile. He didn't look near as tough when he was on a horse as he did with his apron on. From the way he rode I don't guess he enjoyed it much. For his paunch shook up an' down an' his face got red whenever his pony trotted. He couldn't talk at all when we jogged along, but when the ponies was walkin' he had quite a bit to say. "Pretty good-lookin' bronc you're on," he finally says to me. "Looks stout an' looks as if he might make a real cow-horse. How long has he been rode?"

"He don't know much as yet," I says, "for I ain't rode him over a dozen saddles." Then I reached down an' pulled the roan's mane, an' when he slung his head, I felt real proud, for I was watchin' my shadow.

"I used to ride broncs when I was young," he says. An' I sort of looked at him. Just then we started to jog along. I never said a word, but I figgered it must be quite some time ago as I watched his paunch a-shakin'.

'Long about one o'clock we topped a little raise an' come in sight of town. Tex let out a squall you could have heard for most two miles. An' I had the queerest feelin' down my back;

if I'd 'a' been haired over, it would have stood right up on end. The horses, even, seemed to feel the thing, for they all perked up, an' that roan of mine, who had been quiet ever since we left the H's, began to sling his head.

The town looked mighty small at first, but as we kept on ridin' closer it sprawled all over the flat. An engine was smokin' by the water-tank, an' I could see the shippin' pens; an' when we got close enough I could pick out the livery-barn an' wagon-yard where we always put our horses up. An' the place where McDougal lived. There was only one long main street. An' the buildings was mostly 'dobes. What frame shacks there was all had the big false fronts.

But it was two hours from the time we spied the place till we rode down the wide main street. An' we wasn't the only punchers come to celebrate, for the racks was lined with horses.

"The CK's must all be here," a puncher from the H's says.

"There's Tin Cup's Paint," says Tex. With that he let out a squall, an' reachin' down he thumbed his bronc, an' his pony hung his head. There was no need for me to thumb my roan, for the minute Tex's pony hung his head, the roan went to pitchin' too.

Everyone was squallin' now, an'I let out a few myself. I fanned the roan first jump or two, an' I was all set to make a ride, but he fetched up against the rack, an' a bunch of ponies broke loose.

"There goes a bunch of bridle-reins," some puncher says, an' I could hear some others laugh.

Everything was in an uproar now. I was too busy tryin' to keep the roan in under me to see what all was goin' on. But every little while through all that noise I'd hear that squall of Tex's. Finally the roan throwed up his head so's I could look around. Tex was trottin' back to us, for his pony had quit too. Punchers had come swarmin' out to see the fun. An' most of them squalled at Tex. Him an' the H punchers was yellin' back at them as we rode down the street.

I pulled my horse 'longside of Mack, an' he flashed that grin at me. "Well, you an' Tex both showed," he says; then he got quiet again.

I've never felt better 'n my whole life than I was feelin' then. For it's great to be ridin' a big, stout bronc an' know that you can qualify—when you're goin' on sixteen.

We put our horses up in the stable at the lower end of town. Tex an' me had to put them two of ours in a corral out back of the place, for they both had fifteen fits when we rode them inside of the barn. The punchers from the H's left us then, and we had to hunt McDougal up to get some dough to spend. We finally found him at his house, a-settin' in the sun out on the porch. He had us all come in the house while he made us out our checks. Tex said he wanted all of his, an' Mack drawed two hundred dollars. The old man never consulted me; he just give me thirty dollars.

He asked us to stay to supper, an' Mrs. Mc-Dougal asked us too. I think Tex would have liked to have stayed when McDougal's daughter come in. She had been away to school an' I'd never seen her before. But I knowed the other one he had. She was round eight or ten, an' she always rode White Man when she come to the ranch with her dad. First thing she asked was for White Man, for she thought I'd rode him in. An' she was disappointed when I told her I'd rode a bronc.

The old man asked Mack a few questions about the ranch, an' after we talked a little while Mack said we'd better go. The old man an' his wife asked us again to stay. An' I know Tex wanted to, for he was watchin' McDougal's girl.

But she paid no hed to Tex. I seen her sizin'
Mack all up from the corner of her eye, an' when
Mack stepped out on the porch she was still a-
watchin' him. I guess I wasn't the only one
who admired that back of his.

From McDougal's we walked over to the
White House rooms an' got a room with two big
beds. An' after we all washed up an' knocked
off some of the dust, we eased out in the street.
First place we stopped was the Palace Saloon.
An' things was goin' good. The three of us lined
up at the bar, with me standin' in between. Tex
drunk straight whisky, Mack had a cigar an' I
took belly-wash (soft drink). We bought a
round apiece an' I was full of soda-pop. So I
eased on back where a bunch of punchers was
playin' pool. For everybody that knowed Mack
or Tex was swarmin' around them two, an'
everyone was a-buyin' drinks.

I couldn't get no chair, for the place was full,
so I jest stood there watchin' the game an' the
punchers that come an' went. The place was as
big as a good-sized barn, with a bar runnin' half-
way down one side. Acrost from it the card
tables stood, where the punchers was playin' for
drinks. There was a stove at the lower end of
the bar, an' in front of it laid an old tom-cat,

a-payin' no hed to the noise. Back of the stove the pool-tables stood, with the punchers a-swarmin' like flies, an' back of that was the poker room.

I was hungry too, for we hadn't eat but once that day, but I didn't want to eat alone. But finally Mack come on back with his pockets full of cigars. We picked Tex up when we went out, an' just as we was goin' out the door we happened onto Joe, an' Tex made a pass at him an' knocked off his hat. After they scuffled around awhile Joe come along with us. I was for turnin' into the Chink's, for it was the first place we struck. But Tex knowed a better one.

"I'll bet there's a gal a-workin' there," Mack says; an' shore enough there was.

The tables was full, so we rode the stools; an' we all ordered turkey with the trimmin's. Tex was feelin' good by now an' he started kiddin' the girl. But it never bothered her a bit, for she come right back at him. Joe talked some too, but Mack didn't have nothin' to say. There's no denyin' Tex was good.

"How about a little kiss?" he says.

"Go on, you redhead," she says, "or I'll give you a slap acrost the mouth." An' she walked off tossin' her head.

I figgered that she was good an' sore, but in a little while she come on back an' started kiddin' again. Mack paid the check, and when we walked out she was still a-talkin' to Tex.

The three of us went back to the saloon. Joe throwed in with some punchers that was playin' cards. Mack asked me didn't I want to play some pool. We finally got a table, but I didn't do so well, for I'd never tried to play before. An' Mack played pool just like everything else he done. For he spotted me forty-five an' beat me every time. He finally got tired of beatin' me, I guess, for he asked some kid about my size if he didn't want his stick, an' then went on in the poker room.

The kid's name was Rusty but most of the punchers called him Rusty Dirty Hands. He was just about my size, but he said he was seventeen, an' he'd been around a lot. He had wrangled horses at the LFD's an' right now he was working for the O's. I'd stopped once at the LFD's when I was huntin' for work, but I hadn't got a job. I never seen him then, but I guess he had worked there just the same, for he knowed everyone.

Rusty beat me every game at first, an' he never spotted me no balls. But finally I got lucky an' scratched a lot of balls, an' I beat him several times. I shore was feelin' good, for it was Christmas Eve an' everyone was havin' a good time. There was a few fights in the place, but most of them was all too drunk to hurt each other much.

There was some punchers playin' at a table next to ours. An' some drunken puncher staggered up an' tried to pick a fight. But they was all feelin' good an' they just laughed at him. Finally he took a swing at one of them. But he missed the feller he struck at an' fell down on the floor. An' he was too drunk to get back up. So the feller he had struck at picked him up an' drug him over to a chair. He must have hit himself a time or two when he was down, for he was all skinned up some way, an' there hadn't been no blows struck except the one he missed. He called me over to where he was an' asked me did I see that fight. An' I told him I'd seen all of it.

"I'd shore 'a' whipped that bird to death," he says, "if someone hadn't pulled me off of him." Then everybody laughed, an' he wanted to fight some more; but when he tried to stand he fell down on the floor. An' two punchers from his outfit drug him off to bed.

It was gettin' late an' I was gettin' tired an' sleepy, so I went down to our room. My feet was swelled so much from them new boots I like to never got them off.

It was breakin' light when I woke up, an' Mack was already dressed. But he set on the bed an' smoked a cigarette while I slid into my clothes.

We walked up the street to the Chinaman's, an' I took on a big bait of steak an' eggs. But Mack didn't eat no breakfast 'cept coffee an' cigarettes. I wanted to pay the check, for Mack had paid for my supper the night before. But he pulled out a roll of bills that would choke a cow an' wouldn't hear to it at first. I'd never seen that much money in my whole life before, for Mack had won three hundred dollars playin' stud. But when I says I wanted to pay my way along, "That's right," he says. He let me pay the check.

We walked on down to the livery-barn, but our horses had all been fed. Then we went back to the saloon an' played pool again. Rusty Dirty Hands come in. Then Mack made some excuse about havin' to water the horses an' let Rusty have his stick.

The place was pretty quiet to what it was the

night before. There were several punchers sittin' around an' a few was at the bar; the H's
cook was playin' with the old tom-cat. Rusty
had a lot to say about the night before, an' I
got stuck for every game. But I didn't mind it
much, for I had plenty of money. We played till
nearly noon, then me an' Rusty went an' eat, for
I didn't see Mack or Tex. Then we went to the
stable an' saddled up, an' rode out to where the
contest was to be held an' waited for it to start.

There was several punchers already there.
Most of them had bottles an' they was all feelin'
good. Finally Tex showed up with a bunch of
punchers from the O's, an' he was lit for fair.

He throwed his hat under my roan bronc an'
squalled. Next thing I knowed, I was on the
ground, an' the bronc was headin' for home.
None of them made no move to ketch my horse
except Rusty Dirty Hands, an' I figgered it was
good-by horse an' saddle, for Rusty didn't have
a chance on the horse that he was ridin'. But
he happened to run him past a bunch of punchers
just comin' out from town, an' one of them gathered him.

The contest was what punchers call a jack-pot
ropin'. Each puncher put up so much, an' they
roped for the entrance fee. But none of them
made any time that day, for most everyone was
drunk; an' Tex fell off his horse before his steer
had left the chute. No one seemed to care much
whether he caught his steer or not. An' after a
puncher roped they augered for mebbe an hour
before they turned another steer out. Mack
didn't do no ropin' an' he wouldn't ride any
broncs. But he kept time for the ropin' an' he
helped as a pick-up man.

Tex finally ribbed up a deal between Rusty
Dirty Hands an' me with the punchers from the
O's. Each one of us was to ride a bronc an' each
one was to rope a steer. I'd never tried to rope
a steer before, an' Tex lost his twenty-five.

Mack let me ride his horse, an' I must have throwed twenty loops at that old steer, for I finally run him plumb off without ketchin' him. But Rusty caught his steer the second throw an' finally tied him down.

The bronc that Rusty rode was a little hook-nosed bay. He tore Rusty's shirt off of him an' throwed him the second jump. I had an easy one; he was small an' didn't jolt me near as much as the roan that I was ridin'. Tex got his money back on that, but he wasn't satisfied. He bet twenty-five that I could ride the bay that throwed Rusty Dirty Hands.

I wasn't so shore.

Mack saddled him for me, an' just before he turned him loose he says: "Stay in there, kid. Don't try an' make a show, for he jumps pretty crooked. Just keep a-settin' deep in the wood, an' I think that you can ride him."

I'd have been all right, I guess, if I'd stuck to what Mack said, for the pony wasn't any harder to ride than ones out at the ranch. But I was goin' so good I started kickin' him. That was where I made my big mistake, for he got an inch on me an' I never could get it back. Each jump he made he'd get a little more, an' I kept on gettin' higher in the saddle. Finally I seen that

I was gone an' I made a grab for the saddle-
horn. Next thing I knowed I was settin' on the
ground with both hands full of dirt.

It was dark before we all got back to town.
I eat with Mack again; Tex had got clean down
by now, so Mack put him to bed. Rusty an'
me played pool awhile, but I didn't stay up long,
for I was tired an' after I stood around some my
feet was both on fire.

Tex was dead to the world when I come in.
But at that he didn't have much on me. I wasn't
drinkin' either, but jest stayin' in town had me
all done plumb up. For as soon as my head
touched the pillow I was sound asleep.

CHAPTER X

Movin' On

RUSTY DIRTY HANDS was asleep. His hat was pulled down, so's it covered his face, for the flies was pretty thick. He was wearin' his boots outside his pants, an' we both had our feet on the cushions in front of us. For we had a double seat in the smoker all to ourselves. I was rared back in the seat 'longside of him. An' I felt pretty good, for I was eatin' crackerjack as I watched the country floatin' past outside. We had left the big grass flats behind, for we was in Arizona now. The country looked pretty rough to me, an' there was lots of cactus an' pear. At times the dust boiled up an' sifted through the car so's I couldn't see outside.

Between the dust an' crackerjack I was gettin' pretty dry, so I stepped over Rusty Dirty Hands an' walked to the front of the smoker to get a drink of water. A Mexican woman was ahead of me a-waterin' out her kids. So I bought some belly-wash an' oranges of the butcher instead, an' carried them back to our seat. Most of the people in the cars was Mexican an' most of them had kids. I give a kid an orange who set acrost the aisle from us, an' his mother smiled an' spoke to me in Spanish, but I didn't know what she said. I thought she was an old woman till she smiled, then her whole face lighted up an' she looked young. But as soon as the smile had faded off, she looked old an' tired again.

Rusty was still asleep. The dust was so thick I couldn't see outside. But after I drunk the belly-wash an' eat some oranges I felt pretty good again, so I rolled a cigarette an' got to thinkin' of the things that had happened in the last few months. For it was the middle of May right now, yet it didn't seem like any time since Mack an' Tex an' me had rode into town for Christmas, with me on the big roan bronc.

Mack an' me had stayed four days in town. An' I was give' plumb out when I got back to the ranch. For just walkin' around an' losin' so much sleep in town was harder than fightin' broncs. Tex never come back until after New Year's an' he didn't stay long then. For he hadn't been back a month till a horse fell on him an' broke his leg, an' Tex was through with fightin' broncs for good—at least that's what he said. For he'd gone over to the O's, when he got so's he could ride again, an' went to punchin' cows.

I didn't even know where Mack had gone. For he'd bowed up an' quit while me an' Billy Moore was workin' on the water up at Pidgeon Springs. I guess the old man felt pretty bad at havin' Mack pull out for he wouldn't talk of it. The boys said they'd had an argument over some peeler Mack put on. If I hadn't been up at Pidgeon Springs that week I'd have quit an' gone with Mack, for I liked him better than anyone I'd ever knowed. Even more than I did Tex.

Funny, Mack never told nobody where he was goin'. But that was just like him too. For he was always a lonesome kind of cuss. An' he was always on his own. From little things he'd said at times I knowed he'd been around. Once when he told me how they broke horses in Old Mexico, I asked him if he'd ever worked there, an' he had nodded his head. "Four years," was all he said, an' he never spoke of it no more. Then one night after Pretty Dick had been airin' his paunch about Canada an' tellin' what good

horses he had rode up there I was all het up, but
Mack says: "Button, the ponies is always better
on the other side of the hill."

McDougal's would never be the same to me
now that Mack an' Tex had gone. I'd done
pretty well to stay there for three months without them two around. If Mack had stayed, I
don't guess I ever would have quit, for the ranch
had come to be home to me an' I was shore feelin'
low the mornin' when I left. I guess no place
is ever quite the same to a man like the one where
he first works.

But McDougal was pretty decent when I quit.
He offered me thirty a month if I'd stay on. An'
he had tried to buy White Man for his little girl,
but somehow I couldn't think of sellin' him.
I'd left him just the same—when McDougal had
said no one but the little girl should ever ride
him an' they'd take good care of him. For I'd
told McDougal I was goin' home to see the folks.
An' I really thought I was until I met **Rusty
Dirty Hands.**

For Rusty had quit the O's. I'd met him in
the saloon just after I left McDougal's house.
An' when Rusty says he was goin' to Arizona
to try his luck, I decided to go along   For I
hadn't bought my ticket yet for home, an' Rusty

had a way of tellin' things: "My uncle owns lots of cattle there an' he'll be glad to put us on."

Mebbe, it wasn't as big a spread as Rusty said it was. For I knowed that anythin' that Rusty says was more apt to be the truth if you cut it in two. Rusty was all right, though, if he wasn't like Mack or Tex. But just the same, as I watched him snoozin' there with the flies a-buzzin' round, I wished it was Mack instead.

The dust was thinnin' down, so's I could look outside again. Finally the old train stopped, an' the Mexican woman an' the kid acrost from us got up an' left the car. A bullet-headed hombre with a black mustache was waitin' on the ground. They walked on over to a little shack, the only one in sight.

Them little shacks of the section-hands struck me as a mighty lonesome place to live. Out behind this shack was some little home-made graves. Each one was marked with a wooden cross. An' on one little grave that wasn't only three feet long, some wild flowers was growin' in an old tomato can.

Rusty finally woke up an' walked on up in front of the car to get a drink. An' he come back with some crackerjack an' belly-wash an' we both eat some more. We had left the desert be-

hind an' we was passin' some little farms where
everything was green. The train finally stopped
again, so Dusty an' me got off to stretch ourselves an' show off our high-heeled boots. For
the only folks about the station was farmers from
their looks, for all the world like the ones where
I was raised. There was one kid a-standin' there
who looked to be about our age. He was wearin'
hobnailed shoes an' a old wide straw hat. An'
mebbe he didn't look at our high-heeled boots
an' them broad-rimmed Stetson hats.

As soon as we left the little farms we begun
to see some cattle. But they was pretty scatterin'. An' the only horse I saw was a broom-tail
mare that run out of an arroyo we passed, with
a scrawny mouse-colored colt right at her heels.
Neither of them was throwin' off an' they disappeared up over a ridge that was covered with
brush an' rocks.

We was gettin' up into the low hills now, an'
the shadows was gettin' longer. As far as I
could see was them old burnt hills with no sign
of life upon them—except, mebbe, a jack-rabbit
or two with their old mule ears a-wavin'. An'
just at sundown I saw a mangy coyote a-trottin'
along in the shadows.

Rusty hadn't much to say since he finished

with his nap, but finally he says, "It don't look
like much of a country to me."

There's no denyin' it was rough an' different
from them big grass flats back in New Mexico.
But there was somethin' about these barren hills
I liked—an' that made me feel real satisfied.
For the colors was changin' every time I looked,
an' they never looked the same.

Just before dark we passed a bunch of punchers who was loadin' stock. We only got a
glimpse of them. But the cattle all spooked an'
run as our train went roarin' past, an' the punchers was ridin' to them the last we seen of them.
Rusty an' me both squalled an' waved our hats
till they was out of sight, an' an hour later we
pulled into town.

The place was a minin' town, an' we saw a
heap more miners than cowboys on the street.
We turned into the first Chink restaurant, an'
as soon as we took on a feed we walked on down
the street till we finally come to a saddle shop.
The shop was closed, but the windows was full
of fancy bits an' spurs. We stayed there for
quite a while, a-lookin' them over an' pickin'
out the ones we'd like to have.

The first saloon we went into, there wasn't a
cowboy in the place. But we found an empty

table an' played pool till pretty late. Then Rusty bucked the roulette wheel awhile, but he never had no luck. So we hunted up a room an' got a bed, an' Rusty an' me turned in.

Next mornin' we went down to the saddle shop as soon as we had eat. But the saddle-maker told us that jobs was pretty scarce, for most of the outfits was layin' off some hands as soon as they had shipped. He told us we could bring our saddles down an' leave them in his place, an' after we talked to him awhile we went back up town again.

We found the saloon where the punchers all hung out. An' Rusty an' me played pool again. But Rusty soon got tired of that an' bucked the roulette wheel some more. At first he won an' he got back all he lost the night before. But he kept on a-playin' till he lost it all again an' more besides. I wanted him to quit, an' Rusty said he would as soon as he got back what he had lost. But Rusty never did make another lick, an' first thing he was broke.

He borrowed of me to win it back, ten dollars at a shot. But when I'd got down to thirty dollars I cut him off on that. Rusty didn't like it much, for he was shore he'd win if he only made another try. An' he says we'd be all right

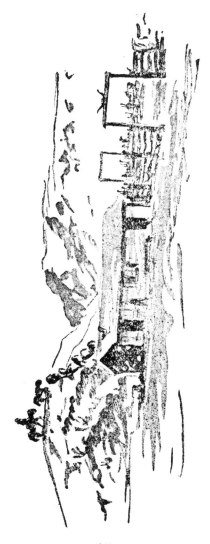

when we got to his uncle's place. But I wasn't
none too shore about this promised job. For
the punchers I talked to in the saloon had all
just been laid off. An' we had to find some
way of gettin' out of town as we was both afoot.

I finally left Rusty in the saloon an' I went
on down to the livery-barn to see what I could
do. I told the hombre who was workin' there
what we was up against. He said there was
two horses that had just come in that the feller
wanted to sell. One was an old stove-up cow-
horse an' the other was just a colt. The feller
who owned them was a lawyer, who had been on
a prospectin' trip. He wanted fifty dollars for
the two of them. But he told me to hunt him up.

At first the lawyer laughed at me when I offered him thirty dollars. But I told him that was
all I had, an' I even turned my pockets wrong
side out to show him I wasn't lyin'. He says the
ponies is worth more than that, an' I agreed with
him. But I says he might as well take the loss
in sellin' them as runnin' up a big feed bill. An'
he finally made out a bill of sale an' told me I
could have 'em.

When I left he says: "If I was you I'd go to
tradin' horses, for there's a heap more money in
it for you than there is punchin' cows." But I

hadn't done so well at that as Rusty an' me found out.

I hunted Rusty up an' told him what I'd done, an' I told him we'd have to leave town right now. For if the ponies eat another feed of grain we couldn't get them out, for we didn't have a nickel to our name. Rusty was pretty low, an' I wasn't feelin' none too well myself—for it was around three o'clock an' we hadn't eat since mornin'. But there was nothin' else to do but saddle up an' leave. An' Rusty an' me pulled out of town a-ridin' on empty stomachs.

I let Rusty take his pick, an' he took the old cow-horse. An' we hadn't gone more than eight or nine miles till my colt give out with me. I walked an' led him awhile, an' then Rusty an' me changed off an' I rode his horse awhile. We kept that up till dark, a-hopin' we'd come to a ranch. But there wasn't no place in sight. Neither of us was talkin' much, so we finally hobbled the old cow-horse, an' Rusty an' me laid out.

Next mornin' the colt went pretty good at first. But 'long about ten o'clock he played out again. So Rusty an' me took turns a-walkin' an' ridin' him till about two o'clock. We found some water then, an' after we all had watered out an' rested awhile we went pretty good again.

But by the time we come in sight of a ranch about four that day, I was walkin' an' leadin' the colt.

We turned our horses loose, an' Rusty an' me both eat until I thought we'd bust, for we hadn't had nothin' since the mornin' we left town, an' we was pretty well ganted up. They told us that Rusty's uncle's place was only a short day's ride from there, an' we both was feelin' good again that night when we went to bed.

Next mornin' I asked the old man who owned the place if he wouldn't trade me somethin' for that colt. The old man looked him over an' finally said he would. For there wasn't nothin' wrong with him 'cept he was too young to ride. An' anyone could see by lookin' at him that he had the makin's of a horse.

The old man said he had a pasture full of spoilt an' locoed horses, an' if I wanted to trade for one of them I could have my pick of the bunch. He sent two punchers out, an' they drove a big bunch into the corral. An' the old man says I could have my pick of any in the lot. Any horse I roped was mine, but once I caught a horse I couldn't turn him loose an' ketch another one. That suited me. Some of the horses they drove in wasn't worth two bits at best. But there was some good-lookin' ponies in the bunch, an' I had my eye on them.

I finally picked out a bay that was packin' a lot of taller, an' I was just ready to take a smear at him when another one caught my eye. He was a bay horse too, an' I knowed if I got my wood on him I wouldn't be afoot no more. He wasn't wearin' any saddle-marks. But I liked that big deep chest of his an' the way he was coupled up. He mixed with the bunch again, an' I had some trouble locatin' him, but finally he come past. I made a smear at him as if I was tryin' to rope everythin' outdoors, but I caught another horse.

Just as my luck would have it I'd snared the sorriest horse in all the bunch. He was an owl-headed-lookin' black—plumb loco too, an' ganted up as if he had never eat. But I had made a bargain, so I had to lead him out.

"If you can't ride," the old man says, "you'd better turn him loose." But I had heard some puncher snicker when they saw me spill that loop. So I figgered I'd show them I could ride, if I wasn't no hand with the rope.

The punchers all played the rail an' waited to see the fun. For they figgered after that loop I throwed I'd never get my wood on him. For

he snapped an' fought his head like any locoed
horse. But I finally got a foot tied up an' got
my saddle on him.

I was still too small to cheek a bronc an' step
acrost that way an' I knowed this one would
throw himself if I used a blind on him. So slippin' a loop around both forefeet I yanked them
out from under him an' throwed him to the
ground.

When I took the foot-ropes off he come on up
with me, but he only made one jump before he
fell. He didn't pitch like any bronc; he just
jumped an' fought his head. An' that locoed
thing fell four times with me, before we got outside the gate.

It was the first time I'd ever seen a locoed
horse, an' it was all new to me. At times he'd
go along just like an old cow-horse. Then all at
once he'd come alive an' kick at his shadow on
the ground an' go to fightin' his head. An' usually when he threw a fit like that he wound up
by fallin' down.

I was afraid he'd get away with my saddle in
one of them fits of his. So I put my rope around
his neck an' run it through the bits, for I knowed
if he ever got away from me, Rusty could never
ketch him on that old crow-bait of his.

CHAPTER XI

Loco Throws a Fit

I STAYED two days at Rusty's uncle's place, then I pulled out by myself. For Rusty had a bellyful of travelin' an' decided he'd stay awhile. Rusty had overshot himself about his uncle's spread. He only owned a few old cows, an' what ponies I saw while I was there looked a heap like my locoed black. His uncle said the only time he put on a hand was when he was brandin' up. But he told us kids we was welcome to stay an' sweat (work for our chuck). That suited Rusty Dirty Hands, but I wanted to find a payin' job. So the third mornin' I pulled out, an' I never saw Rusty again.

I had only gone a mile or so before Loco throwed a fit. An' if I hadn't had a rope around his neck he'd have got off with my saddle. I made up my mind that first chance I got, I'd get shut of him. For he was gettin' on my nerves, an' I figgered that ridin' him alone was much like travelin' with a crazy man.

Rusty's uncle had told me that loco was a weed
an' once a horse starts eatin' it he's never much
good again, for it acted just the same on a horse
as dope does on a man. Some locoed horses, he
says, ain't bad. But he'd seen other ones, when
they come to the water to drink, that would stand
there an' suck themselves plumb full of air an'
never drink a drop. At times they'd stand for
hours at a stretch, as if they was sound asleep,
then all at once they'd come alive an' throw a
regular fit; an' it was almost impossible to get
some of them through a gate, specially if there
was a wire acrost the top, no matter how small it
was.

Some of it sounded funny an' I didn't believe
all he said. But after I'd rode Loco awhile that
day I begun to think that he was right. For I
wouldn't have been surprised at anything he
done. Several times he kicked them old Cross
L spurs of mine, an' anyone to have heard the
noise would have thought I had a buzz saw on my
foot.

If it hadn't been for ridin' this crazy thing I'd
have enjoyed the ride that day. For somehow I
liked them old burnt hills although they was
strange to me. Back on the big grass flats a
man could ride for mebbe half a day an' be in

sight of the ranch. But here the country was changin' every little while an' it never looked the same. After them old grass flats this country looked pretty rough to me. For the hills was covered with burnt rocks an' malpais, an' there was lots of cactus an' pear. Occasionally I'd see a cow or two, but they was pretty scatterin'.

Rusty's uncle had told me I'd find another little spread about twenty miles south of him. But I missed the place some way. I s'pose I was within' a mile of water several times that day, but I didn't know where to look for it. An' old Loco an' me got pretty dry. It wasn't until just at sundown that I come to a little spring. The cattle had tramped it, an' it looked like a big mud hole, but after I dug it out there was plenty of water to drink. I figgered some on layin' out right there. Only there wasn't no feed around. But I watered old Loco out, an' we rested until the moon come up—then we pushed on again.

Old Loco had throwed a shoe an', he was pretty tender in one hind foot. But I rode for an hour, mebbe, a-hopin' I'd find some grass for him. It was one of them soft summer nights, an' the moon was nearly full. The coyotes was yelpin' all around. An' if Loco hadn't been so tired I'd have kept a-pushin' on. For there's

somethin' about a moonlight night that always
gets under my skin. But I finally decided I'd
better stop before Loco quit on me. An' just as
I figgered on hobblin' him out, I run onto two
hobbled ponies.

I rode around them a time or two, but I
couldn't read their brands. It was easy to see
they'd had a hard ride back of them, for they was
covered with dried sweat. First thing I thought
of was Indians, for I knowed I was in the
Apache country now. From what folks said
they was harmless, but still I couldn't feel real
shore. For I'd never seen an Apache in my life
an' I wondered what they was like.

I cut a little circle, a-tryin' to find the camp.
An' I happened on to a cow-puncher a-sleepin'
all alone. He had a good bed all to himself an'
he shore was a-sleepin' hard. After I looked his
layout over good I finally says, "Hello!" But
he never made no move, so I pulled my saddle off
an' took old Loco back an' hobbled him out 'longside of them ponies of his.

When I come slippin' back I says, "Hello,"
again. It was evident that he was dead for sleep,
for he never made no move. No use wakin' him,
I thinks, for there's plenty of room for me. So
slippin' off my boots I crawled in bed with him.

As I crawled in bed I noticed a Winchester an' a belt of shells a-layin' by his side, an' it come to me right then I'd took a chance in not wakin' the puncher up. But I was too tired to do much figgerin' an' that bed looked good to me.

Next thin' I knowed it was breakin' light an' he was layin' there lookin' at me. He'd evidently been awake some time an' had me all sized up for he says, "Well, kid, you must have got in pretty late last night."

"Pretty late," I says, "an' I couldn't see no reason for wakin' you for you was sleepin' hard."

At that he sort of half-way smiled, an' finally he says, "Guess we might as well get up an' see what we can find to eat."

"Any time suits me," I says.

We both crawled out an' pulled on our boots, an' after we built a little fire he put on the coffee-pot. He dug out some old dry biscuits from a sack. An' finally a piece of beef. An' after cuttin' himself a steak he stuck it on a little green mesquite, an' cooked it on the fire. I'd never seen no beef like this before, for he hadn't took off the hide. Must be a new way they have of butcherin' in Arizona, I thinks. An' I stood there lookin' at him, till he asked me if I had a knife.

I nodded. "Well, help yourself," he says.

An' I didn't wait for him to speak a second time, for I was plenty hungry. He asked me where I was goin', an' I told him I was lookin' for work. He seemed to know the country pretty well, for he tells me there's an outfit further south an' just what camp they're at.

"Which way are you goin'?" I finally says.

"Oh, up the country a piece." But he didn't tell me where.

"Workin' for one of the outfits near?" I says. He shook his head he wasn't.

There was somethin' about this hombre that I liked an' I was tired of travelin' alone. I told him if it was all the same with him I'd go along with him. At that he sort of looked at me, but he never said no more until I went to cut another piece of steak. An' when I says, "Funny way they've got of butcherin' out here," he looked at me an' laughed.

He made me think some ways of Mack, for he was about his size an' he hadn't shaved in several days an' he was most as black. But on his forehead was several scars that looked almost like a brand. I wanted to ask him how he come by them, but I figgered I'd better not. For I didn't know him very well just yet, an' he might be touchy on that. But in spite of them scars I liked his looks—an' I liked that bed of his. The beef was tender in spite of the hair. An' them dried old biscuits even tasted good, for there was plenty of coffee to wash it down an' he told me to tear right in.

He cooked some extra steak, enough for a good big lunch, an' then he cut the biscuits in two an' told me to take half of them. I couldn't see no use in cuttin' the chuck if I was goin' along with him. But when I mentioned it to him he told me to take them anyway.

We set around awhile an' smoked after we finished eatin', an' when I told him about Rusty an' me goin' broke in town an' how I come by my locoed horse he had a good laugh at it. He asked me plenty of questions about myself an' seemed glad I happened by. But he never put out no information about himself. An' all the questions I asked him about himself he sort of slid around. He was friendly enough all right an' as long as he wasn't talkin' about himself he had plenty to say.

Finally he says we might as well saddle up. So I unhobbled our ponies an' led them in, while he fixed up the bed. Old Loco was so tender behind he couldn't **hardly** move.

"You won't get far with him," he says. When
I dug up the shoe he offered to tack it on for me.
There was no reason for me a-pickin' up the
shoe, for I couldn't shoe a horse. But when he
said he'd tack it on, I was glad I carried it.

It didn't mean much to me right then as I
watched him tack it on. He didn't have any
hammer or tools, so he straightened it out with
rocks. An' he straightened each nail that way.
An' after he tied up Loco's foot so he couldn't
kick he tacked it on with a rock.

I'd never seen no one pack before an' I wasn't
no help to him in tyin' on his bed. But as I
watched him throw the diamond hitch, I realized
there was several things I'd have to learn if I
was goin' to work out here. For he says that
everythin' out here has packs, as it was too rough
to use a wagon.

We rode along for an hour an' finally we come
to a trail. He pulled his pony up an' pointed
towards the left.

"Here's your trail," he says, "an' there's
plenty of water all the way. Long 'bout noon
you'll come to an old deserted 'dobe house.
There's a trail runs up the hill on the right side
of the house. Take it, an' if the outfit's anywheres in the country they'll be at Turkey

Tanks. You ought to make it by three o'clock."
I had figgered on goin' with him an' it sort of surprised me some.

"I'd rather go with you," I says. "I'm tired of travelin' alone."

"You'd better take this trail," he says. "I'm kind of hard to be around at times, an' I'm used to travelin' alone."

"You look all right to me," I says, "an' we'll get along all right." For I hadn't even tumbled to the fact that he didn't want me with him.

"You better take this trail," he says, "for I'm apt to get in some trouble an' I might get you hurt."

"I'll take a chance," I says, "for you look good to me, an' I'd just as soon ride with you until I get a job as hunt one over there."

"Listen, kid," he says. "Ain't I been square with you? I shod your pony for you an' wacked up on the chuck. 'Tain't much, but it was all I had. An' if it means anythin' to you just ride on down the trail, an' if anyone happens to ask you if you seen anyone that looks like me, you ain't seen anyone. That will more than make us square."

At that he turned off to the right without a-lookin' back. It was evident I wasn't wanted, so

I rode on down the trail. I couldn't make him
out. For he had wacked up everythin' with me
an' still he didn't want me with him. Just then
old Loco throwed a fit an' nickered when he fell,
an' when I finally got him straightened out the
stranger was out of sight.

I come to the old 'dobe house at noon an'
stopped an' eat my lunch, for there was a cold
spring bustin' out by some cottonwoods; an'
after I eat my steak an' washed them dry biscuits down I let old Loco graze awhile, as I laid
in the shade an' smoked. A man can appreciate
spots like that when he's travelin' them old burnt
hills. An' as I laid there in the shade an' watched
old Loco pick the grass, I figgered that Arizona
just suited me, even if some of the folks was queer.

About three o'clock I come to the camp at
Turkey Tanks. The outfit didn't come in till
late, but the cook stirred me up some chuck, for
I didn't mention the lunch. An' when he asked
me where I'd stayed the night before, I just told
him I laid out.

I didn't get a job, but the foreman told me to
stay an' rest my pony up, so I stayed in camp
three days. The outfit left at sunup, an' usually
it was late when they got in. So I laid in camp
an' augered the cook, an' he let me play the
coffee-pot, for I rustled water an' wood for him.

He was glad to have someone around, for he was by himself all day.

The second evenin' I was there two men rode into camp. The cook fixed somethin' for them to eat, an' both of them stayed all night. After they finished eatin' they set around an' augered with the bunch. The punchers all seemed to know them, an' I wasn't long in gatherin' that they was officers from their talk.

For one of them says the Passenger had been helt up not over three days back. There was three men in the hold-up, an' two of them was killed. They hadn't got no money, for the hold-up had been tipped off. But the one that got away had shot it out with them until things got too hot for him. Then he made a run for it. They had finally lost his trail, an' the posse had scattered out. The last they had seen of his trail was when he had killed a calf an' had cut out a piece of meat. But he was headed up this way— a tall black-headed guy; an' they even described them little scars that had interested me.

The officers asked every man in camp 'cept me if they had seen any sign of him. An' I was such a button they paid no hed to me. Not that it would have done them any good. But just the same I felt relieved when they rode away next day. None of the outfit had seen him, least that's

what they said. But I have a hunch that some
of them punchers wouldn't have mentioned it if
he'd stayed all night with them. For I could tell
from little things they said after the officers had
left that there was other folks besides officers
they'd rather have in camp. There's always some
puncher in camp whose conscience ain't none too
clear. An' the fact that the outlaw knew the
country so well made it evident to me that most
of them knowed who he was an' where he was
headed for. Anyway they never got him, an' I
was always glad of that.

For it was my friend they was lookin' for, an'
he'd been mighty decent to me. He had shod my
horse an' wacked up on the chuck when he didn't
have none too much. But it still gives me a chill
when I think of the way I slipped up an' crawled
in bed with him. For it would have been "all
day" with me if he had happened to wake up.
He was probably dead from losin' sleep an' figgered he was safe. An' when he woke up an'
found me layin' there asleep he knowed I was a
harmless kid.

But just the same I'd liked to have seen his
face when he woke up an' saw me layin' there in
bed with him. For crawlin' in bed with an outlaw ain't done just every day.

CHAPTER XII

Nesters

OLD LOCO give quite a show the mornin' when
we left camp. For the first thing he did when I
topped him off was to throw a fit with me. The
outfit finally rode away, much as they hated to
miss the fun. For I wouldn't any more get him
straightened out than he'd throw another fit.
An' I was an hour just gettin' him out of camp.

But once I got him out of camp he jogged
along all right, an' it was just as well he did, I
guess, for the country was pretty rough. I was
ridin' an old cow-trail that wasn't much of a trail
at best. An' there was several places we come to
where I set mighty light in my saddle, for if
Loco had throwed one of his fits right here it
would have been all day with us.

161

I found a spring at noon an' me an' Loco had a drink. But 'long about three o'clock my old cow-trail just petered out, an' I knowed I'd missed the ranch. I didn't even see a cow track any place, an' that didn't look so good. For in places the feed was almost to Loco's knees. An' the only way I could figger it out was that there wasn't no water near. We jogged along all evenin' an' just before sundown I spotted some burros off a ways an' I hoped I'd found a camp. But they all spooked at sight of us, an' I knowed that they was wild.

I stopped as soon as it got dark an' hobbled Loco out. An' the feed come almost to his knees. But he was too dry to eat. I rolled a cigarette an' set for quite a spell, but I was too thirsty to enjoy a smoke, so finally I turned in. An' as I rolled up in my saddle-blankets I could see that old Loco hadn't moved from the place I hobbled him.

Next mornin' I saddled up as soon as it started breakin' light. My thirst was all gone when I woke up, but it soon come back with the blazin' sun. An' by noon my tongue was thick. Old Loco was feelin' it too, for he wasn't goin' none too strong. 'Long about noon I found some **fresh** cow tracks, an' that perked me up again.

For I knowed that water wasn't many miles away if I could only find where it was. I was pushin' old Loco up a long limestone ridge, an' I figgered I'd pull my saddle off when we topped out, for he was just ready to quit, when all of a sudden he begun workin' his ears an' started sniffin' the wind. I got all set, for I expected him to throw a fit. But as we topped out I could see the water he'd smelt. For there was water in the canyon, an' it looked mighty good to me.

There was plenty of water here; the banks was steep, but there was several cow-trails runnin' down to it. But Loco wouldn't drink. The banks was too steep for him to drink from there, an' as dry as old Loco was I couldn't lead him down one of them little trails. I even tried ridin' him down to it but I finally give that up. For Loco would stand an' sniff awhile, then go to fightin' his head. I must have worked an hour with him an' I finally found a place where I thought he could reach the water from the bank. An' after sniffin' the water for quite a spell he finally lowered his head.

Old Loco's ears was workin' back an' forth, an' just as he touched the water with his nose he must have seen his shadow. He struck at it with both front feet an' fell off into the water.

The water was deeper than I thought, for Loco went plumb out of sight. I got excited then. I still had my rope around his neck an' I tried to help him out. Twice I got him to the bank. But each time he 'fell back in again, an' finally old Loco drowned.

I didn't know what to do. I might be forty miles from any place, for all I knowed, with my horse an' saddle gone. It was the first time since I left home that I ever felt sorry for myself, so finally I started to bawl. That didn't help things much, so I decided I might get my rig. I slipped off all my clothes an' after makin' half a dozen tries I got my saddle out. I slid into my clothes again an' set for quite a spell. Then finally I piled my outfit up an' walked off down the canyon.

I hadn't walked a mile since I left home, an' before I'd gone a half my feet was both on fire. At times I'd strike a piece of sand an' I made good time in it; but most of the country was covered with rocks that was hard to take, in boots.

I did a heap of thinkin' as I pegged off down the wash. If I hadn't met up with Rusty Dirty Hands in town, I'd be at home right now, with more money than I'd ever had in my whole life before. An' there I was afoot, dead broke, in a country I didn't know. I knowed that all the money in the world wouldn't do me any good right then. But I cussed myself a-plenty as I walked off down the wash.

I'd gone, mebbe, five miles or so an' I was thinkin' of layin' out—for there was water along the canyon an' I figgered on stayin' by it, trustin' to findin' a ranch or camp next day—when I run into some shod-horse tracks. There wasn't over a dozen of them, but from the way the bunch all traveled I could tell that they was drove. So I follered the tracks for most a mile an' finally come to the bunch. There wasn't no wrangler in sight; but I climbed a little hill an' from here I could see the camp.

There was three hard-faced hombres in the camp, an' none of them got excited when I come walkin' in. But they told me to set in on the grub. An' I didn't wait for them to speak a second time. While I stowed the chuck away, I told them what had happened. None of them had much to say, an' I couldn't make it out. I could tell I wasn't wanted, but it wasn't until a long time afterwards I found out what was wrong.

For the three of them was nesters, puttin' on a little work, an' the yearlin's that they had penned that night belonged to an outfit south of them. They wasn't expectin' strangers when I come walkin' in, for they had about twenty mavericks in the corral that had all just been branded. But I was such a kid it didn't mean nothin' to me. An' when I asked them why they hadn't branded up before, they all just laughed at me.

They must have figgered I was harmless an' yet they couldn't be real shore. For my story of a drowned horse might be all right; an' then again it would have been easy for someone to bring me within a mile or two of camp an' let me walk on in to see what I could see. But they finally fixed a bed for me, an' I was glad to stay all night.

Next mornin' they never offered to stake me to a horse. But they had to get shut of me some way. So one of them says he had a burro at his place about four miles north of there, an' if I wanted to take him I could have the dog-gone thing. Anything, I says, was better than being plumb afoot. An' since they didn't offer me a horse to go an' get him, I pulled on out afoot.

I finally found the nester's place an' it was the usual nester's spread. A one-room shack an' one corral. A little spring came bustin' out behind

the house, an' there was tin cans everywhere.
There was no woman or kids around, an' it was
evident he hadn't been there long. For the pine
boards on the shack looked new, an' the tin cans
hadn't rusted yet. I found the burro on a hill
behind the house, an' puttin' a piece of balin'
wire around his nose, I rode him back to my
saddle.

After I got him saddled up, I took down an'
bawled again. For I knowed I'd never get a job
at a cow-ranch if I rode up on a burro. Of
course it was better than bein' afoot, but that
didn't console me much. An' as I'd looked at my
shadow on the ground, I'd think of the time I
rode into town with Mack an' Tex, an' I'd take
down and bawl again.

I worked my way along all day an' that evenin'
I come to a ranch. No one had been there for
several days, but there was plenty of chuck in
the house. I found some jerky (dried beef) in
a sack. An' I put on a mess of spuds. An' I
cooked some fruit an' a pot of frijole beans, for
I was plenty hungry. I knowed the frijoles
wouldn't be done that night, but they'd go
mighty good in the morning. As soon as I got
the stuff all on I walked outside the house.

It was the time of day I've always liked the

best. Long purple shadows was creepin' acrost
the flats. An' cattle were stringin' in an' out of
the water corral as they come for their evenin'
drink. The quail were callin' from all around.
An' out acrost the flat two bulls were talkin'
fight. I pulled the saddle off my jack, an' was
just a-fixin' to hobble him out when I noticed
some horse tracks in the corral. An' right here
I changed my mind. Instead of hobblin' my
burro out I turned him loose instead. For as
soon as I saw them horse tracks in the corral I
knowed I was through with him. For I figgered
I'd ketch a horse from the first bunch that come
in to water.

It was dark when I finished supper, but as
soon as I got the dishes washed I slipped outside
an' hid myself so's I could watch the big corral
gate. I must have waited two hours before I
heard a horse. But they must have winded me
for they wouldn't come no closer. From where
I laid I could make out their shapes, an' hear
their snorts out on the flat, for they knowed
somethin' was wrong. There must have been
several bunches come while I was layin' there,
for one bunch come almost to the gate before
they spooked an' run. An' as they tore back
out acrost the flat they scared the other ones.

I finally moved my place so's I could have the wind on them. But it must have been near midnight before a bunch come into the corral. I waited until they was well inside before I run an' shut the gate. It was too dark to make out what I'd caught, but their snorts as they tore around inside the corral was music to my ears. An' I've never slept any better in my whole life than I did then, for I was through with ridin' burros.

Next mornin', as soon as I'd built the fire an' put on the coffee-pot, I beat it for the water corral to see what I had caught. There was probably fifteen ponies in the bunch. Some of them was mares. But there was one high-headed black that took my eye, an' I never looked no further. I could see from the saddle-marks that he'd been rode. But it had been some time ago, for he was packin' plenty of taller an' he was pretty snuffy. I went on in an' eat, an' after I got the dishes washed an' had shut the house up again I come back out to the corral.

I sized up Mr. Black as I stood there shakin' out my loop. An' I figgered I'd better forefoot him, for he looked to be pretty stout. It was just as well I did, I guess, for if I'd ever roped him around the neck I couldn't have handled him. There wasn't no snubbin' post in the corral, but I finally got him down, an' after I hobbled him in front I let him get to his feet. He stood there plenty quiet as I eased the saddle on. But from the look of that eye of his I knowed I'd have to ride. I figgered he was too big an' stout for me to cheek, so I slipped a blind on him. An' after turnin' the other ponies out of the corral I eased up in the saddle.

I got all set. Then, reachin' down, I slipped the blind on him. He stood there for a second before he broke in two with me. First jump he took I knowed he was the hardest horse I'd ever tried to ride. For in that first jump I thought he'd loosened all my teeth. He was mighty rough, but he jumped straight ahead, an' when he fetched up against the fence he never made no move to turn. Next thing I knowed I was on the ground—with my horse an' saddle gone.

When I finally set up an' looked around, there wasn't no horse in sight; an' if I hadn't knowed it was a horse that had gone through the side of the corral I'd of figgered a freight train done it. I walked on out to see if I'd ketch sight of him, an' just as luck would have it he had fetched up in a pasture.

The pasture wasn't so very big, but there was no chance of me ketchin' him afoot, an' I knowed

if I crowded him real close he'd go through the wire fence. There was nothin' to do but wait until someone happened by. It might be several days at that; but things might be lots worse, I thought, for there was plenty of chuck at the ranch. So I walked on back to the house.

Every little while I'd go back out to see if he was there; an' I waited around all mornin' an' then I cooked some dinner. It was long about two that evenin' when I spied two punchers acrost the flat. But it wasn't until I climbed the windmill tower an' squalled that they finally seen me wavin'.

I told them what the trouble was, an' they said they'd ketch him for me. But after they looked the layout over they was afraid he'd go through the fence. So they finally rounded some gentle ponies up; an' once he mixed with them they

drove the bunch out of the pasture an' penned
them in the corral.

"Well, kid, you picked a horse," one of the
punchers says, "an' if you're man enough to ride
him it's a cinch you're not afoot; but if he gets
away from you again we'll get your saddle for
you."

One of them roped him for me, an' after I'd
fixed my rig again he eared him down while I
crawled on. I knowed that neither of them
thought I'd ride him, but they never said a word.
When they turned him loose he hung his head
again, but he didn't make for the fence. He
made about four jumps with me before he turned
on good. But them first jumps was as high an'
wide as any I'd ever rode. He was bawlin' now
at every jump, an' each time he hit the ground
with me it was as if someone was clubbin' me
acrost the back of my neck. But that first heat
of ours had took off some of his edge, an' I set
deep in the wood.

As soon as the punchers saw I had a chance
they both begun to coach. "Stay in there, kid,
you've got him now."

For a while I figgered I'd overmatched myself
till they begun to yell. I hadn't tried to spur
him none till then. For he was jumpin' so

crooked at times I couldn't see the ground. Now
I raked him acrost the shoulders, each time he
hit the ground. The big jolts was gradually
slowin' down, an' he wasn't hittin' so hard. But
just the same I thought he'd never quit with me
for I was about all in. Then all at once his head
come up an' he broke into a joltin' trot.

As soon as I got my wind all back a puncher
give me his quirt. "Now, sap it out of him, kid,"
he says, "while you've got the black devil licked."

The big black hung his head again when he
felt that heavy quirt. But it wasn't long until
his head come up again, an' he broke into another rough trot. Then one of the punchers
opened the gate, an' the three of us rode out.

"We're workin' for Old Grimes," one puncher
says, "an' this horse belongs to him. I think your
chances of landin' a job is good if you ride into
camp on him. For he's an old spoilt horse that
belongs in the rough string when he's used."

It was the first time since I left New Mexico
I'd felt real good. For these punchers treated
me as one of them instead of just a kid. The
big black hung his head several times before we
got into camp. But by the time we made it in
that night, he had gentled down an' acted like
any old cow-horse would. An' it felt mighty

good to ride along an' watch my shadow on the
ground again. For the black was bigger than the
roan I rode that time when Mack an' Tex an' me
had all rode into town.

CHAPTER XIII

Wrangling for Old Man Grimes

THE outfit was movin' camp. A mile ahead I could see the dust from the herd as it was movin' slow up Nine Mile Wash. The cook an' the pilot was out of sight right now, but they'd been havin' trouble. For there was eight mules packed with the kitchen stuff, an' all of them mules was broncs. Jim Nelson was still in sight with the horses that carried the beds. An' all fifteen of them was strung out as if they was half asleep. Me an' Joe Gordon was trailin' along in the dust from a hundred an' twenty-five saddle-horses. For we was bringin' up the remuda in the rear.

I had been at the Sixes just a week. I wasn't punchin' cows. But at least I had a job. For I

was wranglin' horses now at forty dollars a
month. An' Old Grimes had tol' me as soon as
the spring work was through I could go to
snappin' broncs.

The Sixes was quite a spread. For Old
Grimes owned lots of cattle an' he was easy to
be around. He told good yarns in camp at night,
for he had come to Arizona from Texas when the
Apaches was still out. From little things I gathered Old Grimes was in a hurry when he left the
Lone Star State. An' I often wondered why
he left, but when I spoke of it to Joe Gordon,
Joe laughed an' says I'd better not ask the Old
Man if I wanted to hold my job. For Joe says
the Old Man had heard the owls hoot many
nights. But I liked the Old Man just the same.
His hair was white as cotton now, an' he was
pretty well stove-up. But there was no horse
run too fast for him when he turned off a hill.
For the Old Man still rode good horses an' he
still led all the drives. An' when there was any
work to do he was always up in front.

Most of the punchers in the outfit had been in
Arizona several years. But they had come from
Texas an' New Mexico, so I felt right at home.
Jim Nelson an' Joe Gordon had both worked
with Mack an' Tex. An' Joe told me he had run

horses with Mack in Canada when both of them
was kids. Joe let me sleep with him, for I didn't
have a bed. An' he showed me how to shoe a
horse an' throw a diamond hitch.

For the country was so rough out here that
everythin' was shod. An' it was up to each
puncher to shoe his own string up. The ponies
they cut to me was shod, but two of them had
already pulled off shoes, an' I never would have
got them shod again if it hadn't been for Joe.
He says it just took practice, for he had to learn
himself. But I knowed it would take a lot of
it for me before I was any good. For shoein' a
horse was the hardest work I ever tried before.
I was so slow at it, the pony usually laid all over
me an' give plumb out before I had him plated.
The shoes was put on cold, an' it didn't take most
punchers long if they was shoein' a gentle horse.
An' mostly when they shod a bronc they tied up
one hind foot.

Joe an' me punched the remuda along, an'
they drove without much trouble. It's easier to
drive a hundred head that's broke to it than it is
just one or two horses.

The cook an' the pilot had the mules unpacked
when we come to Nine Mile Camp. The fire
was already a-goin', and the cook was startin'

dinner. The rest of the punchers was helpin'
Jim Nelson with the beds. An' as soon as they
pulled the pack saddles off I turned the bed
horses up the hill. I would like to have stayed in
camp, for it was past three o'clock, but my job
was with the horses, so I had to pull on out.
When they settled down I could come back.

The feed was pretty good right here, an' the
ponies all went to grazin'. We had watered
them out not an hour before, an' they was plenty
hungry. I rode around the bunch a time or two
after they had quieted down. An' as soon as I
made my count an' was shore that none of them
was gone, I went back to camp an' eat.

The punchers was all just layin' around when
I got back to camp. For it was too late to make
a drive that day an' there was nothin' to do but
sweat. A few was puttin' up their teepees an'
Jim Nelson was shoein' a horse. He had finished
with him by the time I was through eatin' an' I
took him back with me. When I counted the
ponies again I found there was two head short,
for two of them broncs had decided to quit the
bunch an' had pulled out for parts unknown. I
found them headin' back towards Tin Cup
Springs. But it was no trouble to circle them an'
drive them back to the horses.

The last two hours of the day was always long for me. Specially, when the outfit was in camp. For there was always a game a-goin'—an' plenty of funny stories. An' I'd ketch myself a-watchin' the sun, an' figgerin' on the time. For I wasn't s'posed to bring the remuda into camp until just before sundown. But the shadows was gettin' mighty long an' the sun was low. So I throwed the ponies together again an' turned them off the hill. An' by the time I got to the camp, the sun was below the rim.

There was a big corral at Nine Mile Camp, an' after the horses had all watered out I drove them into it. Jim Nelson an' Charley Colts was waitin' there for me. Each one roped his wranglin' mule while I pulled my saddle off. My day was over now, an' there was nothin' to do but lay around. I only wrangled one night a week an' then I was on with Joe.

On nights that I was on wrangle, after I brought the horses in, I'd pull the saddle off my horse an' ketch my wranglin' mule. An' as soon as the remuda had watered out, Joe an' me would drive them mebbe a mile or so from camp before we turned them loose—usually up a canyon where the country was pretty rough. For horses stay better in rough country than they do where the country is flat. It was always after dark when we got back to camp again.

Next mornin' the cook would call us long before it started breakin' light. An' if he was feelin' in good humor, we had coffee before we left. Coffee always helps a lot about that time of day. For our mules would be pretty spooky from standin' tied all night. Pinky was the one I rode—an ornery little sorrel. I usually had to neck him to a saplin' before I could get up on him. Joe rode a little mule called Tom Thumb. He was the smallest mule I've ever seen, but he was far from bein' harmless. Joe said that Tom Thumb had kicked his hat off several times when he was sittin' on his back.

"Wait till I get on him," Joe would say, "before you turn that red thing loose." An' once we headed out of camp you could trail us by the sparks. For their shoes upon them old flint rocks was always strikin' fire.

By the time it was light enough to see a horse we'd be several miles from camp, a-throwin' the horses together an' headin' them down towards camp. On the open ridges there's usually a wind that blows just before the dawn. An' it's just about that time the coyotes cut loose. But everything is quiet by the time the sun gets up.

The punchers would all be waitin' at the corral when we got in with the ponies. An' while Joe an' I eat breakfast they'd ketch the horses they wanted. As soon as each puncher saddled up he'd begin a-toppin' off. I always liked that part of it, for it always meant a show. There's seldom a mornin' in a cow camp when some pony don't explode, an' some of the old cow-horses will pitch till they get warmed up.

When the outfit had a night-hawk he held the bunch at night. At the Sixes it was always an Indian. But the Apache don't like the night. Just let an owl hoot close to him, an' he'll let the horses drift; an' you're lucky to have horses enough to mount the men when the ponies come in, in the mornin'.

At Tanks Canyon the country was pretty flat —high juniper mesas, where the horses would drift for miles. The night-hawk was an Apache, an' he quit because he heard too many owls. So each of us had an hour of standin' guard at night.

Mine was from two till three in the mornin'. That usually meant till four. An' one night when I crawled out, a storm was comin' up. It was blacker than the inside of the blackest mule. When Joe woke me up he says the horses was almost a mile west of camp, an' driftin' towards the north. Just as I was toppin' Pinky off Old Grimes stuck out his head. An' the old man come out of his teepee like a snaky steer comes out of the brush. For we was camped on a big old flat with lots of driftwood layin' round, an' when Old Grimes heard the wind a-roarin' he thought the creek was comin' down.

If it hadn't been for Pinky I'd never have found the horses. For when you're ridin' a mule an' can't even see his head there's not much chance of findin' a bunch of ponies. But Pinky went straight to the bunch. There come a flash of lightnin' an' the horses was all around me.

I circled the bunch as best I could an' tried to hold them together. But each flash of light I'd find horses pullin' out, so I rode a bigger circle. It was just time for me to wake Jim Nelson up, an' I was wonderin' how I'd find the camp, when the storm broke all around us, an' the horses started driftin'. There was nothin' to do but trail along, for the rain was comin' in sheets. Occasionally, I'd get a glimpse of the bunch through a flash of light, an' I follered them till daylight.

I didn't know where we was but as soon as it broke light I found we wasn't over four miles from camp at best. I throwed them together an' made a count, an' found I was out ten head. But when I got back into camp Grimes said I was lucky I hadn't lost half of them.

As soon as each puncher was mounted for the day, the ponies was turned over to me. Mebbe Grimes would tell me they wouldn't want a change that day. In that case I'd bring the ponies in at noon an' water them. Or mebbe he'd say they'd want a change at two o'clock, an' to bring the bunch in then. When we was out some horses, Grimes usually sent Jim Bonehead after them. For Jim was a full-blooded Apache an' he was a horse-huntin' fool. It was seldom Jim didn't show up with them by nine or ten o'clock. Then Jim an' I always augered awhile for I always liked old Jim.

Jim had punched cows all his life, an' when it come to workin' stock he had the white man's ways. But Jim still lived in a wickiup an' eat wood-rats just the same. Whenever the outfit camped at Nine Mile or at Alkali, Jim's squaw an' a lot of his relatives always come an' camped with him. They always made their camp off quite a ways from us. An' when the outfit killed a beef it meant a big feed for them. For Jim's squaw packed off every part of a beef we didn't use except the hide an' tail.

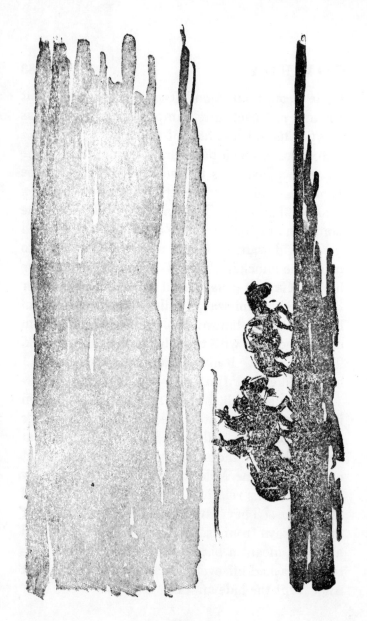

Jim had a scar on his forehead that bothered
me a heap.   One day when we was augerin' I
asked him how he got it.   It seems it was in a
tulapai party an' all the Indians was drunk. Jim
says that T.B. 47 had worked him over with a
club.

"Me sleep long time," says Jim, "then finally
me wake up."

"What happened then?" I says, for Jim's face
cracked into a grin.

"Me cut him a little bit," says Jim.

I guess he did all right, for when I spoke of it
to Joe he said that after Jim got through with
him the only way they could pack old T.B. off
was in a gunny sack.

It was while we was camped at Alkali that old
Jim broke his leg.   They carried Jim over to his
wickiup, for there was no way of gettin' him to
town right then, as he couldn't ride a horse. Jim
never made no fuss, but his face was plenty
white.   An' the Indians made no move to care for
him, but they made a lot of noise.   But Old
Grimes give Jim some pills he said would ease
the pain, an' Jim was dozin' off to sleep when
me an' Old Grimes left.

Grimes told the squaw to keep it up, an' Jim
could get some sleep.   But it was evident they

didn't like the white man's medicine, for they
sung to Jim all night. None of us give the
singin' much, as far as music goes. An' I'll
take the coyotes any time for mine, instead of
an Indian's singin'. But it was evident that it
agreed with Jim, for next mornin' when I asked
him how he felt he said he was feelin' good.

Old Ben, the cook, was up an stirrin' round
two hours before daylight. He usually called
the wranglers when the coffee was on, an' he
squalled at the rest of us as soon as breakfast was
ready: "Come an' get it, you waddies, before I
throw it out." Most everyone played the coffee-
pot first thing when we rolled out. An' there's
always some puncher in an outfit that never eats
no breakfast. I had missed my breakfast several
times since I'd been away from home. But it
was always a have-to case with me, whenever I
missed a meal. For it took more than coffee an'
cigarettes to keep me in good humor.

By the time we had finished eatin', the remuda
would be in sight. Or we could hear the bells
an' the rocks a-clatterin' as the ponies come off
the hill. The wranglers' horses was usually wet
with sweat, for they'd put in several miles. As
soon as the horses had watered out we'd start
ketchin' our horses. An' as soon as each puncher

was mounted the ponies was turned over to me.
I never aimed to take them where they was held
the day before. For a pony likes fresh grazin',
an' he'll tramp out more feed than he eats.

If the feed is good a pony will fill up after he's
grazed a couple of hours. An' if he's on level
ground an' the sun is warm, he likes to sleep
for a while. But if the ground is rough or cold
he won't lay down, but takes his nap standin' up.

When the ponies quieted down I usually beat
it back to camp. If old Ben was in good humor
he'd let me have some coffee, an' there was always some cold steak left over that we hadn't eat
for breakfast. But most round-up cooks is
touchy, an' their feelin's is easy hurt. Sometimes
old Ben was ringy, for lots of times when I come
in he wouldn't notice me.

Mebbe I'd set awhile, a-hopin' he'd relent.
Then I'd pull back out to the horses, with my
empty paunch a-rattlin'. But usually he'd come
through when I drug up some wood, for it's always the wranglers' job to keep the camp sup-
plied. An' old Ben was mighty touchy about
what kind of wood it was. Once he run me out
of camp for draggin' up some juniper. Oak
was what Ben wanted, an' he wanted it solid too.
No half-rotten oak went with him.

Some days I could leave the ponies for hours at a time an' when I come back they'd all be grazin' near. Then again, just let me disappear for twenty minutes, an' there wasn't a horse in sight.

There is always some old rounders in a bunch that is never satisfied. They are always pullin' out for parts unknown when the wrangler turns his head. I had one sorrel in the bunch that was in Old Grimes's mount. Just let me take an eye off him, an' he'd disappear some place. At night when we went into camp he was always the last horse down the trail. Any time the sorrel got some brush between me an' him he stopped. He'd stand as quiet as a mouse till he thought I was out of sight; then he'd pull out the other way till I headed him back again.

Most horses run in pairs, an' they're mighty hard to separate. Some of them run together for years. An' then you'll find other ones that is always changin' off. Old Grimes said that Swallow an' Slipper had run together all their life. Any time one of them was rode an' the other was left in the herd, you'd have thought he'd lost a colt.

Shoestring, Bloucher, and Sailor was never far from each other. When you found one of them

the others was close at hand. On days when the
outfit got in late, a puncher usually brought their
horses out where I was holdin' the remuda. But
whenever Joe rode Shoestring he turned him
loose in camp. An' once he started for the remuda twenty cowboys couldn't head him back.
No matter if the remuda was four miles from
camp, he'd find it just the same. But once he
located Bloucher an' Sailor, he'd go to pickin'
grass.

Leppie was another horse you couldn't drive
away. He had no particular partner; he just
liked to be with the bunch. I wished there was
more like Leppie, for no matter where they left
him he always found the bunch.

Old Grimes had lots of ponies he'd set free—
old cow-horses that had served their time an'
Grimes had pensioned them. But once they
heard the remuda bells when we was movin'
camp, they'd throw right in an' come along, an'
it was hard to cut them out.

Old Wag was the leader of the remuda at the
Sixes. An old stove-up cow-horse that packed
Old Grimes's bed. He didn't look like very
much, but he was the leader just the same. In
the mornin' he was the first horse up the trail, an'
he was always the first one down at night. An'

none of the horses ever crowded him when he
went to take a drink. If they did Old Wag just
raised his head an' flattened his ears, an' they
give him plenty of room.

There's always some fightin' horses in a bunch
an' plenty of timid ones too. Santa Claus was
the worst horse at the Sixes for fightin', but he
never bothered Old Wag. A little bay they
called Deerfoot was scairt to death of the bunch.
He was always the last horse to take a drink
when the remuda watered out. An' unless I
watched him, he was apt to go shy on water. For
he wouldn't drink with horses around too close.

An old cow likes to sup water from a shallow
track. But horses like it deep an' cold. An' I
don't know of a prettier sight than to watch a
bunch water out.

The peeler who breaks a horse is usually the
man that names him. Some are called from their
brands. At the Sixes, Beer-Keg an' Window-
Sash was both named because of their brands.
An' Santa Claus got his name from the pine tree
on his shoulder. Kettle-Belly got his name because of the shape he had. But Slim was a
chunky sorrel an' Shorty was a long-legged bay.
Papago was an Indian pony. An' there was one
gray in the bunch that had lost his tail they

called Central Park. There was Mollie Put the
Kettle On an' a old dun named Parson that they
called Old Methodist John.

The horses in a remuda are all geldings. But
you'll often find one that's named after a girl
some puncher happened to know. An' Pinky,
the mule I rode, had been named after a red-
haired girl in town. In every remuda I've ever
known there's always horses named the same.
There's always a Smoky, an' Skewball, an'
there's always a Zebra Dun.

Next to ridin' fence, wranglin' horses is the
lousiest job in camp. No puncher likes to do it,
for it's kind of a lonesome job. If a man don't
like horses an' ain't interested in their ways, he's
apt to bow up an' quit any time. For there ain't
the excitement in it there is in punchin' cows.
An' the wrangler is usually some old man or a
kid just startin' out. Rain or shine, he's by himself all day. No matter if the rest of the outfit
is all in camp, he has to stay with the ponies.

Naturally I wanted to go to punchin' cows, instead of herdin' a bunch of ponies. But most
punchers serve their time at it when they're first
startin' out. An' I can think of lots worse com-
pany than a bunch of saddle-horses.

CHAPTER XIV

The Baile

OLD BEN was a fiddlin' fool. He said himself
he could play all night an' not play the same
tune more than twice. I don't doubt it none, for
I never heard a puncher call for a tune that Ben
wouldn't cut down on it. Some of them sounded
pretty much the same to me, an' once I spoke of
it to Ben. But he sniffed an' lowed I didn't have
no musical ear, an' as long as everyone else was
satisfied I reckon Ben was right.

There was hardly a night in camp that he
didn't play for us. Someone always helped him
wash an' wipe the tin plates as soon as we had
supper. An' after Ben got the steak for breakfast cut an' we hung up the beef he'd get out that
old fiddle.

"The Arkansaw Traveler" an' "Old Cotton-
Eyed Joe" was two of his favorite tunes. "Hell
Among the Yearlin's" was another one. An'
there was always "Buffalo Gals." Old Grimes

192

always called for "Natchez Under the Hill," for
it was a favorite of his. Sometimes Old Grimes
kept time with the sticks, but all of us kept time
with our feet, an' there was plenty of spurs a-
jinglin'. Most every cowboy sings. He may be
shy on tune, but he's plenty long on noise. An'
in cow camp there's no fear of keepin' the neighbors up, for there's no one but the coyotes to
hear.

Some nights old Ben was ringy when we got
into camp. An' as soon as he cut the steak for
breakfast he crawled into his soogans. But Joe
Gordon knowed every cowboy song that was
ever sung an' Joe done the entertainin'. Joe
knowed verses to the Ranger song I'd never
heard before. Most cowboy songs is mournful.
An' just let some puncher sing "Oh, Bury Me
Not on the Lone Prairie," an' it sets the boys to
thinkin'. Usually they're thinkin' of some cowboy that sung the song in some other camp who
is takin' his long sleep now. For a puncher
knows he's apt to get his any time when a pony
turns over on him.

There was one Joe used to sing we always
liked. It was about a puncher who tried to get
back an' warn the rest of the outfit that the Indians was out. The puncher knows there ain't

much chance of gettin' through, but he takes it
just the same. An' that ride he makes a-gettin'
back would warm any cowboy's heart. For he's
ridin' like a drunken Indian when they wing him
with a shot. He sort of slumps down in the
saddle an' he knows the game is up. He ties
himself in the saddle before he goes to sleep. An'
the outfit gets the warnin' for the pony takes
him through. But the cowboy is dead in the
saddle when the pony brings him in.

Mebbe I'm sentimental; but most cowboys like
that song, for it stands for the kind of a life they
live. An' a cowboy will take a chance.

One night when we was camped on the mountain at Carl Springs an old man rode into camp.
Jim Nelson an' me had to shoe a horse, an' we
come in early that night. The old man was
augerin' with the cook when we rode up. But
as soon as we come in he grabbed his mandolin
an' cut down a tune. He never said a word to
us, but he played for us until we got our ponies
shod an' Ben said we could come an' eat.

The old man took a plate an' set down to eat
with us. We wasn't more than half finished
when the rest of the outfit come in; an' as soon
as they showed up, the old man grabbed his mandolin again an' cut down on another tune. He

played for us all through supper an' never did
finish his meal.

Old Ben was kind of ringy; he crawled in
early that night.   But the old man played until
Grimes shut him off at midnight, an' the outfit
all went to bed.   He played so well Joe Gordon
finally asked him for a song.   The old man said
he didn't sing so well, but he was plenty willin',
and he asked Joe did he ever hear a song called
"Just Break the News to Mother."   Joe 'lowed
as how he'd heard the tune, but quite some time
ago.

The old man started in to sing in a high-pitched, crackin' voice. No cowboy is what you'd call critical, but his singin' was pretty bad. Finally Joe says, if it's all the same to him, he can leave the singin' out an' just stick to the mandolin. An' the old man was plenty willin', for he went on again with his playin'.

The old man was punchin' a burro along with what little outfit he had. And when I asked him where he was from he said Old Mexico. An' he says he's been in plenty of outlaw camps. An' the old man said he had never packed a gun all the time he'd been down there. He was welcome in any of them outlaw camps because of his mandolin. I figgered the Sixes must've looked tough to him when he gave up his supper to play. But when I spoke of it later to Grimes, he said it was probably just a habit with the old man. His mandolin was the only weapon he had. An' his playin' had probably been the reason they hadn't cut his throat.

I've never knowed a cowboy yet that didn't like to dance. They don't often get much chance when they're workin'. But they seldom miss a bet. The outfit was camped at the Big Corral when a stray puncher rode into camp. An' when he says there a *baile* at the nester schoolhouse the next Saturday night, the whole outfit got ready.

Old Grimes was laid up, so's he couldn't go, for a horse had turned over on him. He could hobble around in camp all right, but it still hurt him to ride. But he told me to bring the remuda in two hours by sun, so's we could get an early start. Joe an' me was on wrangle, an' we had to wait till sundown before we took the ponies out. The rest of the outfit was diggin' fresh clothes out of their war bags when I come in. A few of them had washed in the water-hole below the camp. But the cook changed clothes without dippin' himself. An' when he rode off with the punchers he was packin' his fiddle in front of him.

While we was waitin' for sundown Joe an' me both shaved, an' dipped ourselves a time or two in the little water-hole. Joe put on a pretty shirt, an' dolled himself all out. But I didn't have no other clothes, so I only changed my socks. But we both greased our boots with taller before we started out.

Our camp was about twenty miles from the little schoolhouse where the dance was held. An' things was already goin' strong when Joe an' me rode up. There must have been all of forty cowboys there. For the punchers from the Turtles an' the Bar F Bar had all rode in together.

There was ponies tied all around the place an'
lots of them was hobbled. I was ridin' the big
black that night, for Grimes had put him in my
mount. An' he was just the kind of a horse you
couldn't hurt on any kind of a ride.

Joe was ridin' an old wranglin' horse that
Grimes had staked him to, for Joe had nothin'
but good cow-horses in his mount. An' there's
always plenty of extras in a remuda that is good
enough to carry a man to a dance. We finally
located our outfit's horses an' anchored our
ponies with them. An' I slipped a pair of rawhide hobbles on Mr. Black, for he was pretty
salty.

The schoolhouse was pretty small, an' what
with women an' kids around the wall, there was
only room for six couples to dance at once. The
fiddler an' the floor manager was both miners,
an' Joe says that didn't look so good. They was
workin' a prospect close to there, an' there was
lots of miners present. It was evident that it
was their dance till the punchers all rode up.

Most of the girls was nesters an' there was
some big old nester boys. Several of the women
had babies in their arms; there was others on the
floor, an' one corner was sort of penned off just
for the sleepin' kids. Some of them slept right

through the noise, but there was always one a-
bellerin'.

Joe made me acquainted with all the girls.
An' I asked a girl named Annie Brice if she
would dance with me. For Annie was the pret-
tiest girl inside, an' her wrists didn't look so red.
But there was plenty of others ahead of me, for
Annie said I could have the fifth one after this.
I asked two other girls, but they was filled up
too; an' I was just fixin' to go outside when
Annie come to me an' says May Turner didn't
have no partner.

All the girls had ribbons around their waists,
an' May had a big one in her hair. She wasn't
as pretty as Annie, but she could dance all
right. She asked me what outfit I was ridin' for,
an' I said I was workin' for the Sixes. I never
told her I was wranglin' horses, so she thought
I was punchin' cows.

It was hot inside the house, an' I was sweatin'
plenty. An' I wished I had a silk shirt on, while
I was swingin' her around. I had two dances
with May before some miner came an' claimed
her. But she says she liked cowboys better than
she did miners any time. She told me where she
lived, an' I said I might come by sometime. But
I couldn't talk to girls like Tex, an' she done

most of the talkin'. I figgered I'd wait an' see
Annie Brice before I made any dates with May.
For Annie had all the cowboys jumpin' through
the loop, an' mebbe she didn't know it!

Most of the punchers stayed outside when they
wasn't dancin', an' when I walked out they was
ganged up in a circle, for they had a fire a-goin'.
One puncher was standin' with his back to me,
an' I let out a squall. For there will never be
another back like his, an' I knowed him in a
jiffy.

Yep, it was Mack all right, an' I never
knowed how much I'd missed him till I saw him
standin' there. He never said a word at first
but he flashed that grin at me. An' he drug me
off away from the bunch, so's we could talk
alone.

I guess I acted foolish, but I couldn't help
myself. An' at first we didn't even talk; we just
punched each other an' laughed.

"You're fillin' out," Mack says, "an' yore
shoulders is gettin' wider; yore legs is longer
too." But I knowed Mack was lyin' about my
legs, for I'd always be a runt.

"If I'd 'a' been at the ranch that day you left,"
I says, "I'd 'a' quit an' gone with you." Then
Mack flashed that grin again an' give me an-
other punch. An' when I told him about my trip

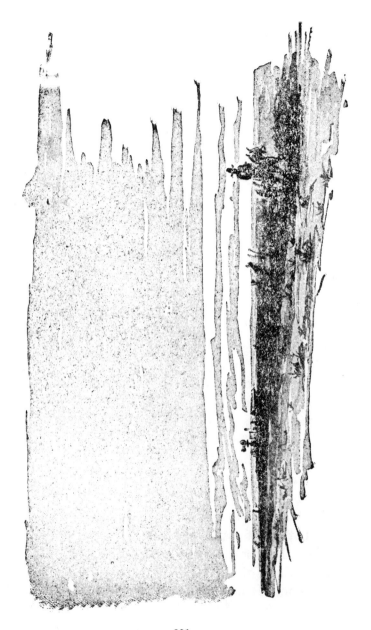

201

with Rusty Dirty Hands an' the locoed horse
he had a good laugh at it. But he got serious
when I told him about sleepin' with the outlaw,
an' said I'd took a chance to ride up on any one
at night without a-squallin' plenty. But Mack
said I done just right in not airin' my paunch
when the officers rode into camp.

Mack said he'd just been driftin' around since
he left McDougal's place. He was up in Ne-
vada 'fore he come down here. But when he
said he was breakin' horses for the Turtles now,
I got a great big kick. For the Turtles wasn't
far from us an' I knowed I'd see him sometimes.
I told Mack I was wranglin' horses.

"Never you mind," he says. "Just keep right
on a-peggin' an' you'll soon be punchin' cows."

It was so good to see Mack again I forgot all
about my dance with Annie Brice. When I
finally hunted her up again she wouldn't speak
to me. So I hunted up Joe an' told him Mack
was here, an' they was glad to see each other.
An' when I told them about missin' my dance
with Annie Brice an' how she wouldn't speak
they both just laughed at me.

Then Joe took Mack inside, an' Mack danced
with several girls an' finally I seen him dance
with Annie Brice, for I was lookin' through the

window. Mack never made no talk with girls like Tex. But they liked him anyway. An' he danced twice with Annie Brice before he come outside again.

Mack told me to ask her for another dance, an' he thought she'd dance with me. I wanted to dance with her all right, so I took another chance. Annie says no girl likes to be left a-holdin' the sack. But she says Mack says it was all his fault, so she let me dance with her.

I tried to talk to her, but she was more interested in Mack than anything I says.

"He's the smoothest dancer I ever seen," she says. I told her he done everything that way even to playin' pool. An' when I told her about the ride he made when the sorrel throwed Pretty Dick she got an awful kick. As long as I stuck to Mack she was interested in what I said. But when I asked her could I come by for her sometime an' take her for a ride she said she didn't know. I asked her for another dance, but she was filled clean up. But when I left she says to tell Mack to come back in again an' she'll cut any dance for him.

As I was walkin' out the door May Turner flagged me down. Here's one, I thinks, that's glad to dance with me. But first thing she asks

is who my tall friend was, an' won't I bring him
in.   I hunted Mack up outside an' told him he
was wanted by all the women in the house.   But
he just laughed.   Mack never danced no more
that night, an' we set an' talked together.

As the night wore on the punchers kept feelin'
better.   For there was several jugs cached out
in the brush.   An' some of the boys was hittin'
them pretty strong.   An' the little foreman of
the Bar F Bar was squallin' inside the schoolhouse, as he swung a girl around.   A tall puncher
from the Turtles finally hung a spur an' fell.
An' they all had to quit dancin' till they got him
up again.   Everyone had a laugh at it, but the
floor manager looked pretty sour.   Finally we
heard the music stop again an' we knowed there
was somethin' wrong.   Next thing it sounded as
if they was shoein' a bronc inside the house, an'
we all run to the windows.

The floor manager an' the little foreman of
the Bar F Bar was goin' round an' round together.   The nester women had backed up
against the wall an' was tryin' to quiet the kids,
for several of them was bawlin'.   But no one
interfered until some miner stepped in to help
the floor manager out.   Then the punchers all
come pilin' in; an' them an' the miners went to it.

I couldn't see very well at the window so I run
inside the house. Just as I got inside I saw the
little foreman of the Bar F Bar spit out a couple
of teeth. But he came right back again an'
knocked a big miner down. Next thing I
knowed Mack was workin' over me outside, for
some miner had knocked me cold.

It must have been quite a fight they had,
judgin' from the talk. For when I was able
to set up an' look around the women an' miners
had gone. Someone had whipped the miner fiddler, an' there was pieces of his fiddle layin' all
about the floor. Mack said the miner hit some
cowboy over the head with it an' busted it all up.

Mack said the miners made a good fight too,
but there was too many cowboys there. He
spoke as if he wasn't in the thing but his knuckles
was all skinned up. Someone had hit Jim Nelson, an' Jim's eye was goin' black. An' Joe
Gordon had a lump over his right ear the size
of a big hen egg. Everybody was laughin' now
about the fight they had. An' the little foreman
of the Bar F Bar was for goin' on with the dance.
So old Ben got his fiddle out, an' the punchers
danced with each other.

The bronc-peeler from the Bar F Bar swung
me around till my head begun to buzz. As soon

as I got loose from him I went outside the house, for my head was still a-ringin' from the wallop that I got. But they kept it up for an hour before the thing all busted up.

When Joe an' the rest of our outfit come, Mack said he'd see me soon. His horse was tied with the Turtles an' I didn't see him again. For there was plenty of excitement now, as we went to toppin' off our horses.

My big black was a-whistlin' when I took the hobbles off. An' I slipped the blind down on him before I eased up in the saddle. An' just as I pulled the blind some puncher begun to shoot. Occasionally I'd get a glimpse of some cowboy a-makin' a ride, but I was too busy tryin' to keep the black in under me to see much that was goin' on. But everyone was squallin', an' there was plenty of shootin' too. The big black fetched up against a Bar F Bar puncher, who hadn't mounted yet, an' his horse broke loose from him. Finally the big black's head come up. An' Joe Gordon squalled for me. All our bunch was all together, an' we left on the run. An' by the time it had started breakin' light we wasn't far from camp.

Joe an' me dropped off here an' throwed the ponies together, an' it was just sunup when we

got to the Big Corral. But Old Grimes had
breakfast ready. Old Grimes was sorry he'd
missed the fun. For everybody was skinned up
some. An' Jim Nelson couldn't see well enough
to rope his saddle-horse. But Jim just laughed
about it. An' as soon as we finished eatin' the
whole outfit started off.

I had the best of it that day, for after the
ponies quieted down I stretched out in the shade
of my horse an' had a good big sleep. An' I
woke up just in time to throw the bunch together an' bring them in at noon. That evenin' I
had another nap, but the boys didn't get a wink,
for as soon as they changed horses again at noon
they made another drive. But that evenin' they
didn't set up long after they finished supper.

I'd slept most all the day, an' me an' Grimes
set up awhile an' talked. An' when I told him
about runnin' on to Mack, Grimes said he'd
heard of him. The old man said he couldn't ask
him to leave the Turtles, but any time Mack
ever quit an' wanted to come to work for him
he'd raise him ten a month. It made me feel
pretty proud the way the old man spoke of
Mack. For he said his kind was mighty scarce
when it come to breakin' a horse.

I told Old Grimes about the ride Mack made

when the sorrel spilled Pretty Dick. An' he said Dick didn't have any business in the corral with some horses Mack could ride. Pretty had worked for Grimes a time or two, when he was driftin' through the country.

The old man finally hobbled off to bed an' left me sittin' there. I was feelin' mighty good when I crawled into my soogans. For I knowed I'd get to see Mack sometimes an' I aimed to tell him what Old Grimes had said. An' if Mack only come to the Sixes to work, an' I caught on as a cow-puncher, there was nothin' else I wanted.

CHAPTER XV

Workin' Stock

SOMETIMES we camped near a pasture, an' whenever we did Joe put the remuda in there an' let me ride with the outfit. Naturally, I was excited. What kid wouldn't be? But I was a long ways from bein' a cow-hand, an' I soon found it out. For I was just startin' in, in a game that takes most a life to learn. An' there's plenty of men who foller it all their life who never do make a top hand. They may learn to rope an' ride all right; but there's plenty of punchers who don't get no further than that.

No man is a real cow-puncher till he's spent years at the game, an' knows what a cow is thinkin' of before she knows herself. Readin' brands an' earmarks comes easy to some men. When we jumped a bunch of wild cattle, if Joe just got a look at them he could tell what there was in the bunch.

Mebbe there might be fifteen head, a-runnin' like black-tail bucks, with several different brands. But Joe would get every earmark at a glance an' he seldom made a mistake; an' Joe knowed when to crowd the critters an' when to give them room, while with me I'd have to whip an' spur an' look them over plenty. An' I didn't know what a critter would do until the thing had happened. The Sixes cropped the right ear an' under-sloped the left. The Six was the only brand Old Grimes was keepin' up. But he owned several other brands he'd bought at different times—each one with a different earmark. An' it's the earmark a puncher goes by when he jumps a bunch of cattle.

There's always some

neighbor's cattle a-runnin' on the range. An'
when a calf is drug out to the fire he's decorated
with the same iron his mammy wears. Usually a
cow will foller her calf when he's drug out to the
fire, or she'll give some sign, so a puncher knows
that the calf belongs to her. But when there's
lots of cattle in the corral they are often sep-
arated.

Joe was a real cow-puncher. By the time he'd
drove a bunch of cattle to the corral he could tell
which calf belonged to each cow. An' as Joe
drug out a calf he'd call the brand his mammy
wore, 'for he knowed every calf by the time we
got them penned; an' once we started to brand
Joe never noticed the cow.

Jim Nelson was a real top hand when it come
to handlin' stock. But Jim couldn't tell a bunch
of cattle at a glance like Joe, nor call a brand,
where a calf was drug out, from just sizin' them
up together as we drove them to the corral. But
when I spoke of it to Joe he says he didn't know
nothin' about stock 'longside of Old Grimes.

Naturally, it was all past me at first, an' like
every kid I didn't know half that was goin' on.
For punchin' cows to a button means nothin' but
ropin' an' ridin'. As long as he gets plenty of
that he's perfectly satisfied. An' he usually fig-

gers because he's wild that he's a regular hand.
A kid can never understand why he's laid off
after the round-up is over an' some old hand is
kept instead, who don't do half as much chargin'.

It's seldom you find a cowboy who is a real
all-around cow-hand. Some of the best riders,
who can do anything with a horse, hardly know
a steer from a cow. An' there's plenty of
punchers who savvy the cow that can't ride a
pitchin' horse. Joe was an all-around cow-hand.
He was through with ridin' broncs, but any time
a pony hung his head with him it didn't bother
Joe. Jim Nelson was a real cow-hand, an' when
it come to ketchin' wild cattle an' understandin'
the nature of a critter Jim was hard to beat.
But just let a pony take two jumps with him,
an' he was shore to spill the pack.

Some cowboys will foller a bunch of stock all
day an' won't know one cow brute from another,
unless there's somethin' unusual about her in her
size or marks or mebbe the shape of her horns.
But to a real cow-hand each cow is as different
as different people is. Lots of times when we
was drivin' a bunch of cattle along, I've seen Joe
ride up on a point an' sit there lookin' at the
bunch as they passed, as if he was half asleep.

Mebbe we'd have two hundred head an' Joe

wasn't makin' a count. But Joe could tell by
lookin' at the bunch if anything was gone. For
after he'd sized them up, sometimes he'd say:
"We're out three head of stock. One is a line-
back cow. I wish you'd get her, Button. I think
you'll find her back towards the second canyon
we just passed. Jim, you an' Wicker see if you
can find the other two. One is a high-horned
steer an' the other one is that droughty-lookin'
two-year-old we gathered on 72 mesa."

He was a real cow-hand, Joe Gordon was, an'
his kind is mighty scarce.

When we camped at Golden Roll I happened
to ask Joe how it got its name, for Warm
Springs wasn't warm at all an' the water was
always cold. Joe says some puncher probably
saw the water smokin' when the snow was on the
ground. Joe says that Golden Roll never had
no name till a few years ago. It was always just
called the camp above Warm Springs, until the
outfit had a cook one fall who burnt the bread all
the time the outfit was there. Joe says his biscuits was shore hard to take, for he cooked them
to a crisp. They was mighty pretty to look at,
but they wasn't fit to eat. Most punchers would
take a bite at them, an' as soon as the cook's
back was turned, they'd throw 'em out of camp.

When the outfit finally moved the brush was full of biscuits.

As soon as the ponies was uncocked we left camp on a trot. We jogged along for a couple of miles with Joe up in the lead. We finally run into some cattle, an' the punchers held them up. I wondered what was comin' off, so I finally asked Jim Nelson. Jim says they work different on the mountain than they do in the lower range. For the cattle was mostly wild up here, an' the country was too rough to make big drives. So whenever they could find some gentle cattle they used them as a hold-up.

"Just set tight awhile," Jim says, "an' you'll see what's comin' off."

We drove the cattle for most a mile before we held them up again. Then Joe took Jim Bonehead an' two other boys an' pulled out without sayin' a word. An' we all just set around an' smoked an' talked for nearly an hour, I reckon. Then away back on the ridge we heard a cowboy yell, an' we knowed that they was comin'. The punchers started cinchin' up an' feelin' of their ropes. An' our ponies, that had been half asleep, begun to sling their heads. An' just as the punchers yelled again, the wild bunch come in sight.

There was twelve head of stock comin' off the hill. But nine was big old steers, all wild as black-tailed bucks. Joe an' the other punchers was campin' on their hocks. An' old Jim Bonehead, the Apache, was a-yellin' every jump.

As the big steers hit the hold-up it slowed them up a bit. But it wasn't but a jiffy till they come bustin' right on through. Ropes was singin' now, an' things happened mighty fast. I managed to get my rope on one big steer an' got my horse jerked down, an' to me the air looked full of hoofs an' horns that was mostly upside down. But Jim Nelson heeled my steer, an' they tied him down before he could hook my horse. When things cleared up a bit so's I could look around all nine of them big steers was tied down on the ground. An' the punchers was sawin' off the tips of their horns, so's they couldn't kill a horse. For each puncher carried a little saw for just that very thing.

As soon as the steers had cooled off some, they drove the gentle cattle around them an' turned the old steers loose. A few of them stayed in the bunch, but most of them had to be roped an' tied down again. There was one old high-horned steer that had to be roped an' tied down four times before he'd stay in the bunch. An' as soon as they had all cooled off we drove the bunch down the country a ways an' made another drive.

The drives was short, an' we kept that up until after one o'clock. Then two punchers held the cattle while the rest went in to dinner. Everyone changed horses as soon as we downed a bait, an' we spent the rest of the evenin' a-brandin' what calves we'd got.

Everybody worked in pairs. Bob an' Jim Nelson was ropin'. Jim Bonehead was markin' ears. An' two punchers was doin' the brandin'. The rest of us was wrastlin' calves. I was workin' with Joe Gordon. For Joe never took the best of it just because he was the foreman. At the Sixes each puncher took his turn at everything. Each day two new men roped an' everyone took their turn at wrastlin' calves, an' no man got all of the ropin'. Joe never played no favorites; neither did Old Man Grimes. An' that was the reason everybody got along an' liked to work at the Sixes.

It takes awhile to learn the knack of handlin' a kickin' calf. For the ropers worked fast that day, an' didn't miss many times. As soon as they drug a calf out to the fire, the wrastlers stretched him out an' held him down, until he was earmarked an' the brand was burned on his hide.

I made hard work of everything, but Joe never
made a move that didn't count. An' by the time
we finished up I was sweatin' as if someone had
throwed me in the crick while Joe wasn't even
puffin'.

As soon as we finished brandin' out, the steers
was cut out an' held, while the rest of the cattle
was turned loose again. The steers was penned
in a corral that night, an' next day they was took
to the pasture.

We worked six weeks on the mountain—
movin' camp every little while. An' the day we
moved down to the lower range they brought us
a hundred new ponies. Joe cut each puncher
six head apiece. An' the ones we had rode on
the upper work was took back to the horse camp
again.

In different countries they work stock different ways. An' in New Mexico where the country is flat they'd throw more cattle together in
one round-up than we'd gather in a week. At
the Sixes the drives was always short when we
was workin' on the mountain, for the cattle was
wild an' the country was rough. It's called
workin' to a hold-up. But on the lower range
we made lots bigger drives, when two men would
hold the cattle up an' the rest went on the drive.

An' on some of the drives at the lower range we branded two hundred calves.

Wrastlin' calves all day in a hot corral, or workin' them red-hot irons with the smell of burnin' hair in your nose, an' your eyes half blind from sweat, comes under the head of hard work. For at the Sixes when they started a thing they always seen it through. An' gettin' back up on a horse again after wrastlin' calves all day was somethin' I always looked forward to. An' some days we'd eat breakfast before daylight an' have nothin' to eat again till that night.

One evenin' we was pennin' some cattle. The sun was just goin' down. We hadn't eat since mornin', an' everyone was thinkin' of supper. Somethin' spooked the cattle, an' they run through the wire fence. An' we all fixed fence until ten o'clock that night, an' didn't get in until midnight. Everybody cussed but no one got swelled up, an' when we got in at midnight the outfit was laughin' an' cussin'.

No two days is ever quite the same when a man is workin' stock. For there's always things a-comin' up that a cowboy has to meet. Sometime a drive works fine, an' you get a lot of cattle. Next time most all of them get away, but it's all a part of the game.

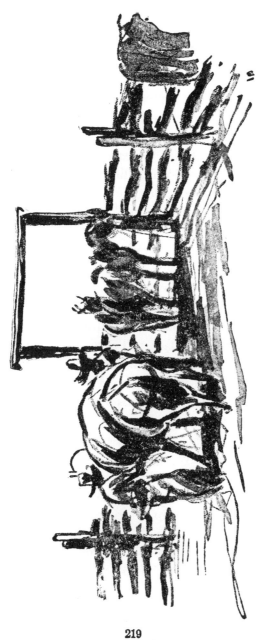

On one of the drives on the lower range Jim
Nelson an' Wicker Bill an' me was all left at the
hold-up.   There was a big flat where we was
supposed to hold up the cattle when they started
comin' in.   There was a little canyon to the left
that was my particular job.   Any time anythin'
come down that canyon I was to throw it out
towards them.

We set around for an hour a-smokin' our cigarettes, an' away back up on Steer Mountain we
could see the cattle comin'.   Occasionally we'd
glimpse a rider a-ridin' for all he was worth.
Then he'd disappear for quite a while an' bob
up some other place.   There was lots of wild
horses up in there, an' we could see them comin'
too.   The wild horses turned off an' never come
down to us, an' afterwards Joe said the way they
was tearin' through the cattle an' cuttin' different bunches back had messed the drive all up.

We must have waited three hours before the
lead cattle got to us.   An' we had all of a hundred head we was circlin' on the flat.   I seen
some comin' down my canyon, an' I went to turn
them out, an' when I got back up on the flat
again all of the cattle was gone.   An' Jim an'
Wicker Bill was tryin' to hold up another bunch.
For cattle was comin' in bunches now, but they

didn't stay long with us. Mebbe we'd circle them awhile an' think we had them stopped. When all at once they'd scatter like quail an' go past us down the country.

Bob an' Joe had been on the outside circle, an' they got into the hold-up as we peddled the second bunch. But forty cowboys couldn't have held them cattle up that day. For they run right over us. So the punchers started ropin' steers as they come past an' a-tyin' the critters down. The rest of the outfit finally come in with their horses wet with sweat, an' the only cattle we had when they got in was tied down on the flat.

There's no tellin' how many cattle come in, in the drive they made that day, but when the whole thing was over we had just eighteen head. An' they was all tied down or we wouldn't have had a steer.

The punchers all let their horses blow, an' everyone fixed their saddle-blankets. Finally Joe laughed an' says, "Let's go to camp an' eat." So we all rode into camp.

"Eighteen head we got," Joe says, an' then he laughed again. "Well, that's better than when we made this drive last year, for we didn't get a steer."

Each day new things was comin' up. An'

about the time I was shore of a thing I'd find I
was mistaken. I didn't know the country yet.
But whenever I went on the drive Joe always
put me between two men who did, so's I couldn't
pull a batter. But any man's first round-up
makes it tough on the rest of the crew. For a kid
is always chargin' around an' doin' things he
shouldn't do.

Every kid likes to rope, an' I was no excep-
tion. But I run more stock out of the country
than I ever roped an' tied down. At times I
thought I was gettin' the worst of it when some
old hand bawled me out. An' I never realized
until a long time afterwards what they put up
with me. For any time a steer broke out, I was
waitin' for a smear. An' instead of tryin' to turn
him back I'd stretch my rope on him.

Old hands may cuss a kid, but most of them is
pullin' for him just the same. If he does the best
he knows. For it takes an old puncher back to
the times when he was startin' out.

Old Grimes rode with us some on the lower
work, but he always stayed at the hold-up. For
the Old Man's days of leadin' drives was through
as he was pretty feeble. Sometimes he'd cuss
when I pulled somethin' worse than usual. But
mostly the Old Man laughed at me when I

pulled a batter. For the old man had been a
wild hand himself when he was young, an' he
liked them kind of kids. An' as long as a man
was a-tryin' he could get along with Old Grimes.

The Old Man told me he "might" let me ride
as a cow-puncher in the fall. That was somethin'
to look forward to, for it meant plenty of ropin',
an' I'd be one of the outfit then, instead of just
a wrangler. An' I'd learn lots from workin'
with Joe—for next to Mack I'd never seen a
better hand than Joe Gordon. I wanted to be a
real hand like Mack an' Joe, that punchers
talked about. An' I figgered I'd make one too,
if I didn't pull somethin' so bad that the Old
Man run me off.

For at times, when I was ridin' out alone, I
begun to feel real old. I was goin' on seventeen,
an' this Christmas would make the third I'd been
away from home. But to Old Man Grimes I'd
always be a kid, I guess, no matter what I done.

It was one evenin' at sundown, when we was
ridin' into camp, the Old Man reined his horse
alongside of mine. I figgered he was goin' to
bawl me out, for I'd pulled a batter that day.
I'd been left alone to hold a bunch of cattle when
an old cow tried to break out. Instead of headin'
her back in the bunch I stretched my rope on

her. The rest of the cattle spooked an' run, an'
when the outfit finally showed up she was the
only one I had.

Naturally I figgered I had somethin' comin',
when the Old Man rode up to me. I could see
him sizin' me up from the corner of his eye as
he rolled a cigarette. I whistled some, an' tried
to look unconcerned as I started coilin' up my
rope. But I could feel the Old Man's eye on me,
an' I got full of panic then. For I figgered
mebbe he'd fire me for what I'd done that day,
an' I hated the thoughts of leavin' the place for I
liked the whole layout. Finally the Old Man
cleared his throat. It's comin' now, I thinks.
An' I dropped one of my bridle-reins when the
Old Man spoke to me.

"Button," he says, "I'd give this whole outfit
an' everythin' I own if I could only be yore age
again an' be just a-startin' out."

CHAPTER XVI

Stampede

THE outfit shipped their second bunch of steers the last of June. They took down a thousand head. Old Grimes wasn't able to ride much yet, so he didn't go down with the herd. Joe Gordon was augerin' the layout though, an' they never had no trouble goin' down to the pens. But old Ben an' me had plenty of trouble all right, goin' down with the saddle-horses.

Old Ben was leadin' the kitchen mules, for they wasn't broke to drive. An' I was comin' along behind him with the outfit's saddle-horses. We was only takin' two ponies apiece an' the horses that packed our beds. An' we wasn't over a mile from camp when one of them spilled the pack.

It was old Tulapai, a horse that packed Joe
Gordon's bed. An' the minute he felt the bed
a-slippin' old Tulapai bogged his head. That
spooked the rest of the horses. An' they run
over old Ben's spread. An' when old Tulapai
come buckin' through his string of mules, it like
to wrecked old Ben's layout. The bed was under
old Tulapai's belly, an' he finally bucked it off.
But not until there was tobacco an' socks strung
for a mile up an' down the wash.

One of Ben's mules broke loose an' headed
back for camp, an' my saddle-horses went the
other way as if the devil was after them. I run
the ponies for a mile before I finally got them
turned, an' Jim Nelson's horse had lost his bed
when I got them rounded up. Half of the other
beds was loose, an' it took me an hour to get
them straightened out. An' I was just ready to
go an' hunt Jim's bed when here come old Ben's
loose mule.

Ben had anchored the rest of the string an'
he had finally got the loose mule headed back.
An' when he come tearin' through the bed horses,
it stampeded the ponies again. Old Ben was no
place in sight, but I finally caught the mule; an'
after I'd anchored him to a stout mesquite I went
after my horses again. I got them rounded up,

an' we headed back up the country. An' when I finally found old Ben he was talkin' to himself. We tied the loose mule on the string again, an' I finally found Jim Nelson's bed. But I never could find his war bag, an' Joe's tobacco an' socks was gone. Once we got them straightened out again, they went along all right; but old Ben was so ringy the rest of the trip he was hard to be around.

We camped at the Troughs' the first night out, an' old Ben had just got supper ready when the outfit showed up with the cattle. Joe told me to put the ponies in a little trap an' go out an' help hold the herd. I was mighty glad to get away from camp, for Ben was still on the prod. We grazed the cattle till sundown an' then we watered them out. Joe an' Bob Crawford was on first guard, so the rest of us rode into camp.

I was on guard with Jim Nelson. Our guard was from twelve till two, an' it seemed to me I'd just got to sleep when Jim come an' routed me out. Jim had set up drinkin' coffee; he hadn't gone to bed, an' he was feelin' pretty spry. But I was full of sleep. It wasn't until we got out to the herd that I really knowed where I was.

Wicker Bill was singin' "Sam Bass" in a voice that would raise the dead. I figgered he'd spook the cattle he was makin' such a lot of noise. But Jim says the cattle like singin'.

"Not that a puncher's voice is soothin' to their ears as some foolish folks thinks," Jim says. "But when a cowboy's singin' to the herd at night the cattle knows where he is. An' when they're asleep they're a heap more apt to scare an' run if a cowboy rides onto them, an' he's not makin' a noise."

Wicker an' his pardner went to camp, an' Jim an' me rode round the herd. All of the cattle was quiet an' most of them was layin' down. It was my first time at standin' guard, an' I asked Jim what I was supposed to do if the cattle spooked an' run.

"Ain't much anyone can do," Jim says, "but trust to God Almighty that his pony don't stub his toe." That sounded sort of scary to me an' I wondered about my horse. I knowed Gray Buck was an old cow-pony, but I hadn't rode him much. I felt better when Jim spoke up again: "Gray Buck has been there lots of times an' he shore savvies the cow. If you knowed as much as that pony does, you'd be a cow-punchin' fool."

Jim was singin' acrost the herd from me, an' I tried whistlin' some. I was plenty awake by

now, for I wouldn't have been surprised at any
time if the cattle jumped an' run. I'd heard
stories about stampedes that raised my hair on
end. The cattle was layin' quiet, an' when Jim
stopped to auger me I asked him if he'd ever
been in a shore-enough stampede.

"Plenty of them," says Jim, "but they're never
half as bad to be in as they are to talk about."

"Ever seen a puncher tramped to death?" I
says.

"Can't say I have," says Jim. "But I've seen
several punchers break an arm or leg when his
pony stubbed his toe."

We rode around the herd some more, but they
all was layin' quiet. A few was up a-walkin'
round. But we never had no trouble, an' Jim
an' me was augerin' when our relief showed up.
We rode on back to camp, an' I was soon asleep.
But it was still dark when we crawled out again
an' went to drinkin' coffee.

They moved the herd off the bed ground as
soon as it was breakin' light. Two of the boys
helped Ben an' me pack up, an' we pulled out
with the horses an' soon left the herd behind.
We never had no trouble an' that evenin' about
four o'clock we come in sight of the shippin'
pens, an' Ben an' me unpacked.

The Turtles was shippin' too, so we made our camp with them. I was for ridin' out to their herd when their cook said Mack was there. But there was wood an' water to rustle, an' I had to look after my ponies too. So I didn't see Mack till supper time when he come in to eat.

Mack shore looked good when he come ridin' into camp. He was ridin' a big bay bronc, that he hobbled when he got down to eat. He flashed that grin at sight of me, an' as soon as he filled his plate he come over an' set by me. I told about what Old Grimes had said about comin' to work at the Sixes an' I was disappointed when I see Mack shake his head.

"I'd like to come," he says, "but it wouldn't quite do. I've got some young horses started an' we're gettin' along all right.

"I'll tell you, though," Mack says, "what you an' me will do as soon as the fall work is over. Us two will take a hunt. I know a place where I'm pretty shore you can get a bear. It's a good place to hold our horses an' there's lots of turkey in there."

Just then Joe Gordon rode up an' told me to put my ponies in one of the shippin' pens an' ride out to the herd. For the punchers hadn't eat since mornin', an' they all had appetites.

The Turtles was holdin' their cattle a mile
north of where we held our herd. Jim Nelson
an' me held our cattle while the punchers went
in to eat. The herd had been watered out, an'
they all was grazin' pretty. When the first
guard come to relieve us there was a new moon
in the sky. An' Jim says if things went as
smooth as they had the night before we'd have it
pretty soft. Jim says that cattle that has been
watered good an' has a paunch full of grass ain't
apt to give much trouble—but still a man could
never tell.

Mack had gone when we got into camp again.
A Turtle puncher told me he ought to be in by
ten o'clock. I was pretty sleepy but I figgered
I'd wait up for him. But I didn't get to talk to
him again, for the Turtle punchers had trouble.

About ten o'clock a puncher come lopin' up
to the fire. He said their cattle was runnin', so
every Turtle puncher got up an' went out to the
herd. I was too excited to think of sleepin' now.
For from camp we could hear the sounds that the
runnin' cattle made. At times it would quiet
down, an' we'd hear the punchers' voices as they
floated acrost to us. Then everything would be
lost again in the rumble of the herd. The Sixes
hadn't had no trouble yet, but one of our

punchers said our cattle was mighty restless when he rode into camp.

Jim an' me both had our horses ready, an' I was for ridin' out. But Jim was drinkin' coffee an' he says to take it easy. But I was afraid I'd miss everything if we didn't get out to the herd.

"Better drink some coffee, kid," Jim finally says to me. "For once we ride out to that lousy herd we'll be there the rest of the night."

I got a cup an' swallered some, but I was too excited to stay in camp an' drink coffee, at the thought of what was comin'. For the sound of them runnin' cattle in the night was too much for me to keep still. But Jim just set there— drinkin' coffee an' puffin' his cigarette. I tried to roll a pill myself, but I was shakin' so I didn't make much of a job of it. An' just as I started to roll another one Mack rode into camp.

Mack's face was covered with blood and dirt, an' his bronc was cut up some. Mack said he wasn't hurt himself, an' as soon as he got off his horse he went to lookin' the pony over. But he wasn't long in pullin' his saddle off an' ketchin' another horse. While he was changin' horses he told us what had happened.

Somethin' had spooked the cattle. He didn't know what it was. For the herd was all layin'

quiet at the time. But they lit on their feet
a-runnin'. Mack an' Dell Woods had been up
on point when they hit a barb-wire fence. An'
Mack cussed barb-wire a-plenty, for Dell's pony
had broke his leg. One of the Turtles' top horses
it was, an' Dell had put a .45 slug between his
eyes, to put him out of his misery.

So Mack caught an extra horse for Dell an'
loped on back to the herd. The cattle had all
been quiet while Mack was changin' horses. But
just as he topped his pony off we heard them
runnin' once more. Mack flashed that grin as
the noise of the runnin' herd come floatin' acrost
the flat to us.

"Guess I better be gettin' back," he says, "for
they're a-rattlin' their hocks again."

"Guess we'd better be ridin' too," Jim says,
"for the chances is good we'll be needed before
so very long."

As we left the light of the camp I couldn't see
a thing. But by the time we got out to the herd
I was makin' out pretty good. The new moon
had sunk below old Turnbull Peak. But the
stars was crackin' overhead an' there wasn't a
cloud to be seen.

"Fine night," says Jim, a-puffin' his cigarette.
"We're lucky it ain't a-stormin'."

Our herd was a mile to the south of where we had left them when we went into camp at supper time. An' the punchers was ridin' close herd on them, for the cattle was all on their feet. We couldn't hear the Turtles from here. But there was somethin' in the air all right, an' even the ponies could feel it. For old Gray Buck, as gentle as he was, begun a-slingin' his head.

Wicker Bill an' his pardner didn't go back to camp when Jim an' me rode up. An' Joe Gordon was the first puncher I run acrost as I rode around the herd. Joe had been with the cattle ever since dark, an' his pony was a-limpin'.

"I'd like to change horses," Joe says to me, "but I don't want to leave the herd. Hell's goin' to be poppin' pretty soon, an' all of us will be needed."

I knowed I was the most useless person there, so I offered to let him have Gray Buck while I went in an' changed for him. I made the change in mighty quick time, for if the cattle stampeded I wanted to be there to see it. Now that I was on a horse an' movin' around I wasn't excited so much. It's settin' in camp a-waitin' for things that makes a man squirm. An' Joe an' me had just swapped back again when our cattle spooked an' run.

Gray Buck was an old cow-horse that had been there plenty of times. As soon as the herd all started old Gray Buck broke into a run. Next thing I knowed we was up on the point an' I could feel the ground a-shakin'. A thousand wild-eyed steers was headin' into the night an' headed for the devil knows where.

It was a funny kind of noise they made that's hard to put into words. Someone was ridin' ahead of me; I couldn't tell who it was. He finally turned an' squalled, but I couldn't tell what he said. No man's voice could carry above the roar of the herd. Their horns made a clickin' sound that was different from the roar of their feet. An' there was the crackin' sound the cattle made whenever they hit some brush.

An' I could feel old Gray Buck's heart a-poundin', up against my leg. There was other punchers 'longside of me now, an' the leaders begun to turn. Someone had pulled his gun; I could see the flashes when he shot, an' it give me a funny feelin', for the gun didn't make a sound. The ground was pretty open; I was mighty glad of that. I was only hopin' we didn't hit no wire fence. But as far as excitement goes it was the best I'd ever had. It made toppin' a pitchin' pony off seem like a kindergarden game.

It's hard to tell how far they run when the leaders begun to circle. Not over a quarter, Jim Nelson says, but I thought it was twice that far. As soon as the millin' started I figgered the cattle was through. But Jim says they was millin' too close, an' they'd soon bust out again. Their horns was crackin' now as they milled an' churned about. I figgered we'd lost at least half of them, but it was the way they was jammed.

They finally busted out and broke into another run. But the whole outfit was ridin' to them now, an' they started millin' again. At times they'd quiet down for a while, then they'd spook an' run once more. But by the time it started breakin' light they was pretty well quieted down. An' Jim an' me held them alone while the outfit went in to breakfast.

They didn't look much like the steers we held the night before, for they was pretty well ganted up. Some of the old leaders had their tongues run out a foot. An' lots of them had bloody heads where they'd busted off a horn. Naturally I was all steamed up, for I'd been in a real stampede. But when I started to crow to Jim he only laughed at me. For Jim was an old cowhand, an' nothin' excited him.

"Shootin' that gun was a sucker trick," he

says, "whoever pulled the stunt. An' the fact
we got them to millin' showed they wasn't so
very wild." Jim seen he'd let me down, for I
wasn't feelin' so cocky.

"Well, I enjoyed it anyway," I says, "an'
there was enough excitement for me."

"Of course you did," he says, "an' I got a kick
myself. But people who tells stories of stampedes where cattle runs forty miles in a night,
with dead cowboys an' horses strung all of the
way, is only spillin' the bull. For the worst run
I ever seen, when daylight come we wasn't over
five miles from camp." Jim had let me down
considerable, so I didn't say nothin' more. An'
when the punchers come to relieve us we rode
into camp an' eat.

When they counted the bunch out that
mornin' we was shy ten head of steers. But
Wicker Bill found six of them not over a mile
from camp.

Everyone changed horses when they went into
camp. An' as soon as the cattle was counted
they started workin' the herd. The cattle was
classed an' inspected long before nine o'clock.
We loaded ahead of the Turtles, an' I didn't see
Mack again, for he was off huntin' a bunch of
steers the Turtles had lost.

We prodded the last steer in the cars 'long about two o'clock, an' as soon as we finished eatin' we started packin' up. Joe asked me if I wanted to go to town with the boys. But I didn't have much money comin', an' Jim Nelson said he'd bring me a bed from town, an' I knowed when I got the tarp an' the soogans paid for I wouldn't have much left, so I said I'd go back to the ranch. But I wanted to go to town all right when the bunch pulled out. Even old Ben was smilin' as he rode off with the punchers.

Joe an' me took the horses back to the ranch an' I was feelin' pretty low. But when Joe says Old Grimes was goin' to let me ride this fall if I made out all right with the bronc I broke, I was feelin' good again. For I figgered I'd be a real cow-puncher then an' be through with wranglin' horses. For what little cow-punchin' I had seen looked like more fun to me than just a-breakin' horses.

I told Joe what Jim had said about the cattle runnin' an' how he says it wasn't much of a stampede.

"It was good enough for me," Joe says, "an' I'm plenty satisfied that there wasn't nobody hurt. If we wasn't all a-ridin' to them we'd have lost a bunch of steers."

I didn't tell Joe about the hunt that fall, for that was between Mack an' me. After we'd jogged along for an hour or so, both of us quit talkin'. An' I was asleep in the saddle when we finally got to the ranch. The sky was showin' gray in the east by the time we got unpacked. So Joe an' me never wasted no time a-crawlin' into our soogans.

CHAPTER XVII

Mack Breaks His Last Bronc

JOE cut me ten head of broncs, an' Old Grimes
played the fence while I was workin' with them.
The Old Man pretended he liked the show, but
he never fooled me none. The Old Man knowed
I could ride when I rode into camp on the big
black horse, but he wanted to see how I handled
a pony. For there's plenty of peelers who can
ride anything that can't learn a young horse
nothin'. I reckon Old Grimes was satisfied, for
as soon as I got that bunch snapped out, Joe cut
me ten head more. An' the Old Man seldom
come down to the corral; he'd just set in the
shade on the porch.

The Old Man had got plenty of falls in his

life. But this last one had just about finished him. There was mornin's when he could hardly get out of bed. But the Old Man never complained. He'd set for hours on the porch in that rawhide-bottom chair, a-starin' off acrost the flats with a far-away look in his eyes.

Cows an' horses was all the Old Man knowed. He seldom talked of nothin' else. He had took his land from the Apaches an' he'd held it with a gun. The Old Man had never married an' he'd lived pretty hard; but every cowboy liked to work for him, for Old Grimes was square.

The night the outfit come back 'from town Jim Nelson brought him two bottles of Old Crow. An' after the Old Man had a few drinks he begun shootin' at flies on the ceilin'. An' he kept his old .45 hot till all of his shells was gone. It shore was funny to the rest of us, but nobody said a word. An' what laughin' we done we did outside the house. For the Old Man was layin' on his bed a-puttin' holes through the ceilin' an' we could hear the Old Man squall each time he hit a fly.

The outfit never come back till after the Fourth an' they didn't stay long at the ranch. They soon pulled out 'for their different camps, an' only Joe an' Jim Nelson was left. Them

two packed salt till the summer rains come, an'
then they doctored for worms. Old Grimes
didn't keep a cook only when the outfit was
workin'. Old Ben an' Wicker Bill an' two other
boys was buildin' a trap on the mountain.

Old Grimes was a fool about a horse, an' one
day when Joe an' me was goin' to the horse
camp after some ponies he says if we seen Baldy
an' old Blue Dog to bring 'em back with us. I
didn't know the ponies, but Joe says they was
two old horses that Grimes had pensioned an' set
free. Both ponies was close to thirty years old,
an' Grimes had broke both of them, an' no one
but him had ever rode them from the time that
they was broncs.

Both ponies was old stove-up cow-horses but
they was packin' plenty of taller. The Old Man
says to put them in the alfalfa patch where we
kept a wranglin' horse. An' he would set for
hours just a-watchin' them two old ponies.

On days when Joe an' Jim was gone, as soon
as we finished supper I'd set out on the porch
with him, an' Old Grimes would tell me stories.
It was the time of day I always liked the best.
For the cattle would be stringin' into the water
corral, an' the big flats was covered with shadows.
The quail would be callin' from the hills an' some

old bull would be a-bellerin', an' back on the open
ridge another would answer him.

Old Grimes told me stories of the old-trail
herds—an' of cowboy fights in town—an' how
the Comanches come in with the light of the
moon an' stole the settlers' horses. The Old
Man had gone up the trail from South Texas
when he was just sixteen. When there wasn't
a wire fence from the Gulf of Mexico clean to
the Northern Lights. I always figgered there
was plenty of open country yet, till the Old Man
got strung out. But when he spoke of buffalo-
hunts an' Indian fights I knowed I was born
too late.

As soon as I'd gone to work for Grimes I'd
wrote a letter home, an' when Jim Nelson come
back from town he brought me a letter from
mother. One night when Grimes an' me was
settin' out, he asked me if I'd answered it. I
made some pore excuse at bein' no hand at writin'
an' not havin' any paper. But that didn't go
with Old Man Grimes, for he hobbled inside an'
brought out a pencil an' a tally-sheet, an' made
me write to mother.

"I put it off myself," the Old Man says, "until it was too late."

The rains was late that summer an' the spring

had been pretty dry. The Old Man was gettin'
anxious, but he never said a word. I'd ketch
him a-watchin' the thunderheads as they come
boilin' up each day. I was ridin' with Joe an'
Jim these days, a-diggin' the water-holes out.

At Tin Cup Springs we had to fight the cattle
back while we scooped an' dug with our shovels.
An' none of them got half enough, for Tin Cup
was nearly dry.

There was plenty of feed back in the hills
where there wasn't any water. But only the big
steers could range that far, for they traveled like
saddle-horses. Most cows can't range as far, an'
the feed that's closest to the water is always eat
off first. Comin' from the big grass flats I wondered what the cattle eat at first, for there wasn't
a spear of grass. Then I seen them a-pickin'
at the browse an' bush, but they all looked pretty
thin.

"This outfit's blowed up," Joe says, "if we
don't get rain pretty soon."

It began to show on the punchers too. Not
that we was sufferin' any. But a man can't work
with stock, where there's no grass for them to eat
an' their eyes sunk for want of water, without it
showin' on him. Joe and Jim's faces looked
lined an' old, when they come in at night.

One evenin' Wicker Bill come into the ranch after a packload of chuck. He says the water at Mud Springs had just played out, an' things looked bad on the mountain. Bob Crawford, the horse-camp man, was a-waterin' the horses in bunches. Only ten head could water at a time, an' Bob says if it didn't rain pretty soon he'd have to move all the horses.

"I don't give a damn if it never rains," the Old Man says. An' he hobbled inside of the house.

"Don't think he don't," Joe says, when the Old Man was out of earshot. "He's just a tough old mushog that ain't used to cryin' any."

So no one spoke of rain again when the Old Man was around. The Old Man's face was hard as flint, an' he quit tellin' stories. For now, each day when we rode out, we was findin' dead cattle.

It come one day at noon while we was all eatin' dinner. A little patter on the roof at first an' then a regular old washout. We run outside the house an' stood there in the rain. As far as we could see on every side the whole sky was a-leakin'. Joe an' Jim Nelson done a wardance, an' I started squallin' myself.

The Old Man's face had softened up, but he never had a word to say. But he was standin'

there, with the rain a-pourin' off his face, with
both hands stretched towards the sky. It wasn't
till we finally went inside the house that the Old
Man spoke. "I didn't mean that, what I said
that day, about it never rainin'."

That was all Grimes ever said. But that night
as we all set on the porch, the Old Man says the
way Baldy an' Blue Dog was kickin' up their
heels in the alfalfa made him feel young again.

It rained more that night. An' next mornin'
when I wrangled the horses on the big flats,
where there hadn't been nothin' but dust, the
green had begun showin'. An' the old burnt
ridges was a-showin' green on them. It rained
again next evenin', an' the next day, an' the next.
An' when it had kept it up for a week I wouldn't
have knowed the country.

The big flats was covered with filaree with the
purple flowers a-showin'. The ridges was covered with a carpet of green. An' the hills was
ablaze with poppies. The ribs still showed
through the pore old cows. But the white-faced
calves was playin'. Their mammies was too busy
pickin' the grass to pay much hed to their
calves. There was water in all the canyons now,
an' on evenin's when we set out on the porch Old
Grimes told stories again.

247

The first rain we had there was no lightnin'. But it made up for that later on. Most punchers is afraid of the lightnin', for in the hills it comes pretty strong. An' when the lightnin' starts poppin' on the limestones most punchers make for a canyon. It was funny to watch Joe an' Jim whenever we was out. They was both afraid of storms an' they wasn't slow to admit it. I'd always liked a storm till one day when we got caught. An' I thought it was mighty funny that Joe an' Jim was scairt.

We had two pack-mules with us an' was headin' back for the ranch. An' they was a-poundin' the mules on the tail to get in ahead of the storm. We was comin' up one of the long ridges just a few miles from the ranch. The clouds was a-boilin' all around, an' they was green over towards Mescal. An' every time Jim rolled his eye that way he'd pound a mule on the tail.

The storm broke all of a sudden, an' at the first sharp crack overhead, Joe an' Jim both left me with the mules an' fogged off into the canyon. I was soakin' wet in a minute an' I figgered I'd go on—for the water was runnin' down my back, an' my boots was full of water. The lightnin' was poppin' all around, but the rain was to our backs, an' me an' the mules was makin' time till we hit the limestone ridge. I thought that I'd seen storms before, but right there I changed my mind.

I wished I was in the canyon along with Joe an' Jim. The flashes almost blinded me, so I shut my eyes. Occasionally, I'd open them for a squint ahead. Little sparks was showin' at the tips of the mules' ears, an' each time I touched my pony with my hand it made me think of strokin' an old tom-cat's back an' a-watchin' the sparks it made. We finally made it into the ranch in the middle of the storm. An' Old Grimes cussed me plenty for travelin' the limestone ridge.

I had the mules unpacked an' was all dried out by the time Joe an' Jim showed up. Both of them had been watchin' me as I went up the limestone ridge. They said at times we'd disappear an' they figgered we was done. Then we'd show up for a minute, then disappear again. There's no denyin' I was scairt, but I never let on to them. I just told them it wasn't as bad as it looked from the bottom of the canyon. But I made up my mind right then an' there, I'd never be caught on a limestone ridge in a storm a second time if I knowed anythin' about it.

As soon as the rains come on, the screw-worms come; an' we was ridin' early an' late. I wasn't much hand at ropin'; but I always went along, for it was a good way to try out the ponies I'd broke. I had to go easy with them. I missed lots of ropin' because of them broncs, for I couldn't ride them too far. After I'd rode one a few miles or so, I'd go back an' change to another.

Screw-worms is caused from a blow-fly. At least, that's what Grimes said. The fly lays its eggs in a cut or sore, an' next thing it's full of worms.

The first day I was out with Joe an' Jim we doctored a big old steer. Somethin' had hooked him in the side an' he had a bad case of worms. They held him up with some cattle on a ridge, for he wasn't very wild, an' they was figgerin' on drivin' them down on the flat before they stretched him out. I was ridin' one of my broncs an' had a big loop cocked. I was hopin' to get a smear at him if he come out past me. An' as luck would have it I got a throw, for the cattle spooked an' run.

I made a lucky dab an' caught him goin' off the hill, an' things begun to happen. For I'd never roped outside of a corral; I didn't know

enough to give him slack an' foller him off the
hill. There was a big flat below us too, but that
meant nothin' to me. I didn't even get my pony
straightened out before he hit the end of the
rope.

We went three ways at once, an' the old bronc
got jerked down. If it hadn't been for Joe an'
Jim I'd have been in a fine jack-pot. For as soon
as he got to his feet my pony went to buckin', an'
about the time he got strung out real good the
steer would jerk him flat, for the rope was tied
to the saddle-horn. An' I'd caught the old steer
around the neck.

I finally set up an' looked around, but it sort
of dazed me at first. Joe an' Jim was laughin'
fit to kill. When they finally stretched out the
steer, we got my outfit straightened out an' I
watched them doctor the steer. Joe poured some
worm medicine in the wound till all of the worms
was killed. An' after he dug the dead worms out
he covered it with black oil so's the flies wouldn't
blow it again.

The old steer was on the peck when they
finally turned him loose, an' we'd of had another
show if it hadn't been for Joe. For the minute
the steer got up he charged my horse, an' the
pony went to buckin'; I figgered he'd get hooked

sure. But Joe dabbed his rope on the steer an'
turned him end from end. An' I got my old
bronc out of the way before they turned him
loose again.

I was still a tenderfoot when it come to
handlin' cattle. I'd always worked with the
horses an' I didn't savvy the cow. Usually when
I done a thing I managed to do it wrong. But
I was learnin' one thing mighty fast—that there
is lots more to bein' a cow-puncher than just
settin' on some good pony an' lettin' your feet
hang down.

One evenin' just at sundown I was ridin'
towards the ranch. I was ridin' one of the open
ridges an' enjoyin' all the sights. The white-
faced calves was a-playin' an' their mammies
grazed close by; an' two bulls was havin' a fight
up the ridge a ways.

It was nip an' tuck with both of them. If one
of them give a foot of ground he got it back
again. Their heads was close together an' their
tongues was lollin' out. The ground was torn
up all around, for they'd been at it quite a while.
If I'd known then what I do now I wouldn't
have rode so close. For the minute a bull sees
he's got the worst of it he ain't long in runnin'
away. An' once he starts, he starts right now,

for he knows the bull he's fightin' will hook him if he can. I've seen bulls that was caught in their getaway turned plumb over when they was hooked.

But this night I was ridin' a gentle bronc an' I got pretty close. I'd never seen a good bull-fight before, an' these bulls was matched pretty even; I shore was enjoyin' the fight. One of them was finally givin' ground, an' I was figgerin' he was licked, when all at once he turned an' knocked my pony down a-makin' his getaway.

He didn't know where he was goin', but he was on his way. He hadn't seen the horse, an' it would have been all the same to him if he'd headed towards a big brick wall. The other bull was after him. Both of them crashed off the hill an' disappeared in the brush. It never hurt me any but I had to walk into the ranch, for once the pony got to his feet he left for camp on the run.

The outfit could see me comin', so they knowed I wasn't hurt. When a loose horse with a saddle on comes tearin' into camp the boys ain't long in back-trailin' him, for usually a man is hurt.

The four of us had finished eatin' one night when a Turtle puncher rode in. Joe was helpin' me braid a cinch, so we didn't go outside. But I knowed there was somethin' wrong when the others come into the room. Nobody spoke at first; then the Old Man cleared his throat.

"I've got some bad news, Button. A pony turned over on your friend Mack, an' he'll never ride no more."

Somethin' pinched me in the throat an' I wanted to go outside. But the Turtle puncher was talkin', so I kept my seat on the bed.

"We never heard him mention his folks an' we figgered you might know, for lots of times he spoke of you an' another puncher named Tex."

I couldn't trust myself to talk, so I finally shook my head. I was thinkin' back to the ride Mack made that day when the horse throwed Pretty Dick. An' of the Christmas we spent in town.

"I knowed him ever since he was a kid," Joe says, "but I don't know where he was from. Nobody ever knowed him very well, I guess—when you come to think it over."

"It happened several days ago," the Turtle puncher says. "He was stayin' at the Turtle horse camp by himself a-breakin' a bunch of broncs. Two of us rode in this mornin' an' found them both in the corral. The pony had evidently been pitchin' an' broke his neck when he fell. Mack must have been caught in the riggin' when the pony turned over on him. For the saddle-horn had caught him in the chest an' he had never moved."

Somethin' choked up inside of me an' I stumbled out of the house. An' I was down in the corral alone when Old Man Grimes come out. He set down alongside of me an' smoked awhile before he spoke.

"It's all right, kid," he finally says. "It's somethin' we all have comin', an' if Mack could have had his choice he'd have probably took it just that way."

The Old Man never said no more an' we set for quite a spell. At last he got up an' hobbled to the house an' I follered the Old Man in.

I was always glad they never took Mack into town. They put him to sleep on one of the hills that was miles from anywheres. I think he'd like that too—where there wasn't no one near. For he was a lonesome kind of cuss an' he was always on his own.

CHAPTER XVIII

I Make a Hand

IT was the latter part of August. We had moved up to the horse camp an' begun to gather horses for the fall work. For several days the punchers had been stringin' in. Old Grimes wasn't able to ride that fall, an' Joe was still augerin' the spread. As soon as the ponies was gathered he cut each puncher his string. He cut each man six head, an' we started shoein' up. The horse camp was a busy place with fifteen punchers there.

Old Ben was cleanin' up the Dutch ovens an' skillets, an' matchin' the kiack boxes up. Punchers was goin' over pack-saddle riggin' that hadn't been used since spring. Bed-rolls an' saddles was layin' about. Punchers was laughin' an' cussin'. Everybody was feelin' good, an' the ponies was fat an' sassy.

The night before we pulled out for the river, Jim Bonehead rode into camp. An' Jim brought another Apache named George who was to jingle the ponies that fall. It was a big relief to me when that Indian come ridin' in. For I was afraid I'd have to wrangle horses again if he didn't show up pretty soon.

Next mornin' we crawled out with the mornin' star. Old Ben had breakfast ready. As soon as we finished eatin', the pack-mules an' the bed horses was roped, an' we started packin' up. Wicker Bill pulled out with the pack-mules as soon as they was ready, with the cook at the end of the string. Jim Bonehead follered with the bed horses.

Then Indian George opened the big corral gate, an' the remuda begun stringin' out. The punchers begun toppin' off their ponies, an' there was plenty of fun right then. But everybody managed to stay right side up as the outfit rode out of the gate. It was my first time out as a cow-puncher an' the fall work had begun.

The End